if
not
now,
when?

if not now, when?

the many meanings of black power

by
Dora Pantell
and
Edwin Greenidge

DELACORTE PRESS / NEW YORK

CONTENTS

if
not
now,
when?

1.
BLACK
POWER

It was on a hot June evening in 1966 that a comparatively unknown young Negro, brooding over the attempt to kill James Meredith during his lonely Mississippi march, shouted, "We need to stop all this singing and get us some Black Power!" The pronouncement, blasted over radios and television sets across the nation, set off a mood ranging from appalled shock and panic at one extreme to foreboding exultation at the other.

Both emotions may have been justified. The white man has since watched aghast while embattled blacks attempted to march on a Miami national convention or killed policemen in cold blood in Cleveland; shuddered at actions which seemed to be inventing a new morality to take the place of his system of law and order in the Ocean Hill-Brownsville demonstration school district in New York; and wondered, as he observed the black revolution move on to apparently ever more extreme postures, about who was really the underdog in the United States today. The Negro, in the meantime, his standards increasingly determined by "what is good for the black man," has begun to develop a sense of group solidarity fully committed to the acquisition of black power through demands or explosions—whichever, from his point of view, would appear to be more productive.

Actually, the concept of black power emerges legitimately from the original organization of our democracy or, going back still farther, from the ideology of the New World settlement. With the possible exception of the earliest colonial town halls where each man was his own advocate, American government has always been a structure of delegated responsibility. Elected representatives, normally men of sense and sensibility, usually found it wise to accommodate themselves to the needs and interests of those who put them in office.

The black power theory, as expressed by Negro historian E. Franklin Frazier more than twenty years ago, had at its core the need for adequate political representation for the black man. The enlightened white liberal, ever eager to stretch the limits of our democracy, extended his understanding, his cooperation, his energy, and his checkbook to the cause. But times have changed. The very meaning of black power has become fragmented. Black extremists resent both the presence and the proferred aid of the eager, loving Whiteys. Only breast-beating whites move among them now to suffer humiliating insults. Most white people find in this strategy of hostility another strong reason for distaste and alienation from the black revolution.

Extremist black power tactics are deliberate and purposeful. The program seems to have a twofold goal: the discernible separation of the extremist black from other militant Negroes—most definitely from civil rights workers—and the severance of the Negro tie of dependency on the white man.)

The first goal is evidently more a matter of style than substance. Unforgiving stares, harsh, frequently obscene language, and a condescending refusal to make any distinction between "good" whites and "bad" usually mark the behavior of the black extremist. It is a daring style, meant to exasperate the white man and to prod the black. In both respects, it seems to be successful. Certainly, it has been much copied by other less violence-oriented Negro groups.

The second black extremist objective, that of breaking loose from dependency on the white man, is largely segregationist in philosophy. The thinking envisions black communities, even black states, able to develop a self-sufficient capacity for production and management, and capable of providing full employment and education for their people. It anticipates the possibility of conflict with the white power structure through programs for self-defense. It intends to use any means, regardless of how destructive, to "overcome."

(This grandiose design was never part of Martin Luther King's dream. Nor is it—yet—the ambition of the vast majority of the approximately twenty-one million embittered blacks living in the United States. They hope for what must sometimes seem equally doubtful of fulfilment—a fair representation in the political life of the country.)

The definition of fair representation excludes the

politicians whom blacks call "white" Negroes and those they derisively describe as having "settled." A white Negro is one who fails to identify with the suffering and the hopes in a disadvantaged black community. He may be a middle-class Negro whose tastes and interests find a closer identification with middle-class whites—or blacks. He may never have had other than a bond of blackness with his less fortunate fellow Negroes, and he may prefer not to dwell too much on this accident of skin coloration. He may, in the process of moving up to a better life, have forgotten—or taught himself to forget—how it felt to be a poor black man in Watts or Harlem or on Chicago's South Side. Or he may remember too dimly and have little patience with the fumblings and incoherencies of uneducated blacks as they try to verbalize their demands or with their insistence on saying their piece —which he knows by heart—because they need this evidence of acceptance. All such detached Negroes are white in the opinion of a poor black community and as non-representative of their interests as a white man is, occasionally even more so.

A Negro who settles usually starts out with a commitment to his ethnic community. But all through his political life, he has choices to make. He can, for example, in the councils that plot a city power structure, hold out for a black man to head a department concerned largely with Negro needs; or playing the more amiable part of the cooperative Negro, he can acquiesce to the appointment of a white man. He can, when discussing projects intended for the welfare of black people, communicate their concern about participating in the planning, or absorbed in mainstream ideology, he can forget about their involvement until he is ready to present them with the finished product. He can make his own decisions, or afraid that political machinery will find ways to get rid of him, he can let the party make his decisions for him. Thus, he settles for leading parades, for changing the names on street signs, for cutting ribbons at official ceremonies, for delivering the sermon on the white way of doing things to his people, for—finally—utter powerlessness as far as the poor black community is concerned.

⟨The black ghetto dictates the definition of fair representation today—for clearly, it is a black ghetto revolution that America is involved in during this second half of the twentieth century. It is the poor and the uneducated blacks of the ghetto who have risen to shout—or to burn—for power. To those who are still hopeful enough to refrain from the burning, power means representation that will be responsive to the needs and concerns of poor black people.⟩

(Moderate black militants—as distinct from black extremists and from the traditional moderate Negro— see in this struggle for power within the existing structure of American society the foundation for a permanent solution of the "Negro problem." They denounce separatism, whether it takes the form of white supremacy or black segregationism, as a tool in upholding the doctrine of racism which Negroes have the greatest stake in destroying. They argue against violence even when they know it is an expression of unendurable despair. And they assume the responsibility of working in the ghettos to help the people achieve the education and community organization upon which all social change must ultimately rest.

The stress of the moderate black militants is on involving the black ghetto rebel in working out his own destiny. Federal legislation has provided for ghetto representation in all Office of Economic Opportunity anti-poverty programs. Wherever such programs have been started, moderate black militants strive to develop indigenous leadership, operation, and control.

It is no easy task. Communication is often difficult. Ghetto rebels—as all revolutionaries, probably—have their own taboos. An educated person, even an educated black person, is suspect. His very use of correct English sentence structure is often enough to brand him as an outsider. The ghetto has no faith in outsiders. They have for too long turned their backs on poverty. Their intercession now is regarded as an intrusion into hopes which they cannot understand and as the usual attempt at manipulation with vested interest answers.

Excesses are frequently difficult to contain. Apathy in black communities has largely given way to arrogance. The taste of power is sweet to those who have long been denied self-determination. Demands may be unreal, overreaching. And failure to satisfy them may well leave a hostile community vulnerable to the injection of racism. The conflict at Intermediate School No. 271 in the Brownsville section of Brooklyn grew out of the action by Rhody McCoy, the local unit administrator, to "dismiss" nineteen teachers and supervisors from his district, after approval of Community Governing board. The action was opposed by the Superintendent of Schools and by the United Federation of Teachers on the grounds that employees thus discharged, have been given no access to hearings or other provisions of legal due process. The leadership that stepped into this breach did so with unmistakably militant tactics. Ousted teachers and principals were refused access to their rooms (though directed to go there by the Superintendent of Schools), schools were closed, and children herded into an auditorium where they were led in a chant of "Black Power! Black Power!)This school is OURS!"—an expression of possessiveness, perhaps important for the sake of self–pride, but much more likely to encourage students in thinking of their teachers as enemies than to promote either educational progress or helpful black-white relationships.

It seems depressingly obvious that ghetto blacks do not have enough faith in a democratic society to reach out to it for help through more orderly channels. The feeling among people who have worked with them in the growing number of poverty-represented councils, committees, executive and governing boards, is that they must first have the confidence that their own point of view has been fully heard and respected. Much time may be lost in the process, but the monologue—this time by the black man—must evidently precede the dialogue. The relegation of power must also apparently come before complete readiness for it. An unqualified ghetto representative running for office as chairman or recording secretary of a local governing board, for example, rarely admits his unfamiliarity with the duties involved. But once having savored the triumph of victory, he may well feel free enough to ask for help. Recognition is undoubtedly a basic component in education for democracy.

Efforts to help black people use legitimate democratic institutions for the development of representative and responsible black power are admittedly uneven. Anti-poverty or community action programs are not flourishing everywhere. Some Southern states are loath even to permit their admission to a community, and when through one means or another they are persuaded to do so, often supply staff virtually guaranteed to impede success. One such program, organized to upgrade Negro literacy, hired an embalmer with a total of six months of teaching experience—in an unrelated field—to be its chief educational consultant. And Southern Negroes, as a rule gentler and more diffident on their decadent home grounds, are sometimes slow to change. But even the most backward among them know that a revolution is brewing. They may participate actively in the battle or they may watch it from the sidelines, but there can be no question about their sympathies.

Moderate black militants take heart from the growing number of middle and upper-class blacks who are joining the ranks. The exclusiveness of elegant black country clubs has not entirely shielded affluent Negroes from the knowledge that to white America they, too, are a once servile people who have not yet earned the right to full equality. They work now in the black moderate camps, helping to organize, to publicize, or to raise money for the common cause.

It is in the interchange between these blacks—and here and there, some whites—who have achieved and the ghetto blacks that perhaps the greatest hopes of the moderate black revolution lie. Harry Belafonte may sing for the future of his people but he may also lick stamps and address envelopes, if he is asked to. Former football star Jimmy Brown is reputed to earn $200,000 a year as an actor and businessman but in

NAACP or CORE headquarters he may take orders from a welfare client. The humility involved in these relationships is both a boost to the much bruised ghetto ego and an important means of closing the distance between an isolated, violently defensive community and the world around it.

The realism which is so much a part of the black moderate militant movement forces it to admit, however, that substantial success is not yet in sight. Our nation is still stubbornly divided. White society may, for the most part, no longer condone the brutal life of the black ghetto. But neither is it ready to welcome into its midst on terms of democratic equality the product of black poverty. Yet, it is precisely through the powers of democratic equality that the non-violent poor black man views his salvation in America.

Poor people are not always good at expressing themselves. Martin Luther King probably defined their battle for them when he summed up the meaning of a gathering of the poor in Washington. "We have come for our checks," Dr. King stated simply. A militant old black woman may have offered some further insights when she figured, "So many slaves for so many hours over so and so many years! It's a considerable sum the white man owes us. And that's without counting the interest."

The "interest," these days, has many meanings, each associated with a new or differing phase of the black revolution. If this divided country—as the President's "Riot Commission" * reports the national condition— is ever to be reunited, it will not be through easy

* U.S. National Advisory Commission on Civil Disorder

solutions or simplistic formulas. The white man needs first to understand more concretely the hatreds and confusions of the Negro who, when the United States Constitution was written, counted as only three-fifths of a human being. And the blacks, even the extremists, must recognize the equally sick apprehensions and anxieties that drive white people to the protection of the "all deliberate speed" clause which, since its enunciation by the Supreme Court in 1954, has been variously interpreted as postponement, distortion, or only partially subterfuged defiance.

2.
WHERE
DOES IT
HURT?

The average American Negro hurts all over. He is so full of hurt that he may readily see slurs where none are consciously intended and just as frequently bristle with an indignation that the white person finds mystifying. A middle-class black mother, for example, her own children carefully sheltered in a private school, feels personally insulted when a white mother talks to her about disorganized conditions in some inner city public schools. An Afro-American teachers' association rises up in protest when another teachers' association —with both black and white membership—asks that seriously disruptive children be taken out of regular classrooms. The complaint is lodged by the Afro-American group that teacher uneasiness relates to black disruption only and the accusation filed that white teachers want to deny black children their right to an education.

In white circles, this attitude is sometimes referred to as a chip on the shoulder. Introspective Negroes agree, but go on to say that such reactions are only to be expected in a transitional period of the black revolution. The American Negro is still much too uncertain of his status to put any faith in either the white person's gesture toward communication in terms of an equal concern about public school education or in his professional detachment about the special needs of difficult children.

Among ghetto blacks, the insecurity is felt on a different level. The omission by a white person, for example, of a please or thank you may serve as an acute reminder of the authority figure that the white man has always represented. It can evoke with uncomfortable vividness the ancestral memory of the slave owner's lash. The response is far too complex for easy explanation. A ghetto black is largely unaccustomed to analyzing his reactions. His people were for too many centuries discouraged from such personal indulgences.

But he has learned in the past few summers how most effectively to express both his passionate rejection of the historic prejudice that constitutes his underlying pain, and his demands for alleviation of the specific injustices that a democratic society, as casual in its responsibilities to the poor, evidently, as in its social relationships, imposes on him. Breaking of store windows, shooting from roof tops, burning buildings with the home-made Molotov cocktails—they are his way of telling the white man to listen. They are his warnings to the establishment to hear him out while he angrily recites the list of his grievances.

There are apparently more of them than most white people have suspected. And the knowledge that comes from the inside of the ghetto does not seem at all to match the view from the outside.

There is the matter of housing, for example. The public projects stand tall and orderly and impressive. The passing white motorist may resent their number when he thinks of his income tax. But he also feels a righteous satisfaction when he sees how neatly he has disposed of his poor. He has done it very fairly, too. Only the very poor, that is, those whose incomes fall within certain brackets, can live at reduced rentals in public housing. As soon as a tenant earns more than he should, he is asked to leave.

What the white man seemingly does not know is that this siphoning off of those residents who have managed somehow, to summon up enough initiative to better themselves leaves only the unenterprising, unmotivated, totally hopeless poor in the public projects. The more frightened among them are almost literally trapped, their tentative efforts to self-improvement diffused by the overwhelming prospect of higher rents and eventual eviction. There are those, of course, who earn more than they report to the Housing Authority. But over them, too, looms the fear of being found out, evicted, and forced to cope with a higher rental which sometimes makes the higher salary hardly worthwhile. So—the ghetto in the housing project perpetuates itself. Its children, robbed of all models of striving or success, grow up with ghetto standards. Pretty soon, the schools begin to reflect the ghetto picture, too. Public housing is quite definitely not the easy panacea that the establishment hoped it would be.

But, as the black people see it—and they with the Puerto Ricans make up the majority of the tenants in low-income projects—there is still more to be told. Public housing authorities, functioning within the law, give no reason for the denial of an application of admission to the project. They have the further right to evict from a project any mother with a history of out-of-wedlock children, any unattached female involved in an extra-marital relationship, and any member of a family arrested for any one of a number of reasons. They carry out these responsibilities with the same efficient—and often ruthless—dispatch as the sanitary inspections which they make periodically. Their reign of rectitude seems to be on the wane, however. At least in some areas, the white man has begun to listen. Changes in policy may remove moral strictures as criteria in the administration of public housing; or at least modify the standards so that they can be lived up to by ordinary mortals. It is even possible that some day public housing residents may be permitted, like other human beings, to keep a house cat as a pet, if they like.

Of course, no one is forced to live in a public housing project. A poor family may prefer to remain in a ghetto tenement, with an absentee landlord, a superintendent—when there is one—usually off the premises, and a deterioration in living conditions that can perhaps best be highlighted by a statistic. In 1965, there were over 14,000 cases of rat bites in the United States, the vast majority of them in ghetto areas. White middle-class families would not tolerate such a condition for a moment. They rarely have to. Most middle-class whites know the channels of making a landlord accountable to his tenants. Most ghetto blacks do not.

The picture that the black man draws of ghetto health conditions may again somewhat jolt the white man's complacency. In 1965, the infant mortality rate among non-white babies under one month old was

58 per cent higher than among white babies of that age and almost three times as high for babies from one month to one year old. Life expectancy at birth was estimated as 6.9 years longer for whites than for non-whites; at the age of 25, the difference was 11 per cent in favor of the whites. There are no definitive figures to document the reasons either for these differences or for the higher rate of job and school absenteeism usually attributed to minor illnesses among ghetto residents, particularly among blacks. But the lack of ghetto exposure to the health educational process must surely be considered as part of the causation.

Public health education proceeds along many and diverse routes. Information about drugs and medical research appears frequently on the science pages of a number of magazines and newspapers. These are not usually the publications that the ghetto reads. Unless a drug is advertised on the television screen, a ghetto resident is unlikely to hear about it at all. Coricidin, librium, terpin hydrate, household words in middle-class parlance, are unavailable in most ghetto drug stores. Pharmacists see no point in stocking their shelves with items unfamiliar to the community.

Ideas about preventive measures—anti-cold vaccines or innoculations against measles for example—similarly reach the ghetto, where crowded and unsanitary conditions make them most necessary, last, rather than first. On the comparatively few occasions when these drugs are administered in city clinics, doctors rarely have the time to give explanations. Patients may be receiving the best that is available to medical science, but they neither know what is happening to them nor are they able to pass the information along. Public health education is hardly likely to move ahead very fast when general medical information remains a mystique.

Blacks are objecting to the chaotic conditions of city clinics, to the dirt in municipal hospitals, to the beds in the corridors, to the fact that so few of the municipal hospitals are attached to a good medical school. But most of all, they are crying out against the dehumanization in both clinics and hospitals of the person most involved—the patient. His fears and anxieties about what is wrong with him and what can be done to help receive little or no attention. In some parts of the country, psychiatric reports about the effects of anxiety on physically ill Negroes have been received with considerable shock. Blacks are not supposed to have such complicated emotions.

Grievances about sanitation sometimes seem to mystify white communities, too. The tendency is usually either to blame ghetto blacks for creating the mess to begin with or to assume that the black man doesn't care or he would have done something about all the filth long ago. The facts are that city sanitation departments seldom make the number of collections that a dense ghetto area requires, that their pick-ups in such neighborhoods are frequently slipshod—leaving barrel droppings, more often than not, to fall where they may—and that feelings of futility about individual efforts to maintain habits of order and cleanliness in a ghetto contribute both to ultimate inertia and to bitterness, if not depression.

It is also a fact that compliance with the much contested and finally passed Federal rat control bill has, to date, been routine. More garbage is collected but the vast resources of an advanced technological nation have not been put to work to study more effective ways of preventing or eliminating rat infestation. And indeed, why should they be? A black ghetto problem does not call for that kind of investment—except in the minds of blacks. The extremists bring up the subject, time and again, as one of their battle cries.

The grievances about white policemen—referred to as storm troopers or occupation forces in the black community—need no extremist incitements to make them explosive. The average ghetto black reacts to the white cop with just about the same instantaneous fury as the bull to the flaunted red cape. Every ghetto riot in the last several years has started with the presence of a white policeman in a black neighborhood. Even if he does nothing more threatening than to get out of his car—as did the three who were killed in Cleveland in July 1968—he is suspect. He is coming to flail his stick or to "whip black heads."

A white community, accustomed to thinking of the police as the guardians of law and order—and as the nice men who help children and little old ladies across the street—find this incomprehensible. But all Negroes know that a white policeman sees a black man as a troublemaker and that he is treated accordingly. A black community is ready to shout, "Don't you hurt that black man!" even when a white policeman is trying to protect one black from another.

White people find it almost as difficult to understand—or to listen to—the grievances growing out of three other important ghetto problems. These relate to welfare, employment, and what is happening to ghetto children. Each is an inflammatory issue.

The concept of public assistance in the United States has changed over the years. Help that was originally given as a dole has gradually come to be considered, upon the establishment of eligibility, as a right. The controversy between welfare recipients and the larger society here seems to center on the question of exactly what these rights encompass.

National television audiences have lately been exposed to some verbalization from black welfare recipients as to what they believe are their rights. In some cases, the attitudes have clearly reflected the black point of view about retributive justice, to wit: the white man has, through the years, lived high on the hog; the Negro, if he had been given the chance to participate equally in America's economic growth, could have had his share of the benfits of an upwardly mobile society; and in today's affluent life, he is demanding his portion of the gravy. Inevitably, this attitude brings the expected response from the whites with their comfortable liberal self-image: their own particular forefathers never enslaved the American Negro; they, personally, never held him down. Granted, they may unthinkingly have gone along with policies and traditions that kept the Negro in his economic place. They know better now. But nobody in his right mind can be expected to readjust welfare allowances on the basis of retributive justice!

In most instances, nothing quite so drastic has been involved. Welfare recipients have usually complained about "meddling social workers" who "trample on the dignity of the individual." Some Welfare Departments are now separating their social treatment cases from those needing maintenance income only and New York City has initiated the honor system in a few districts where experimentation has shown no greater degree of falsification on the part of families who merely sign an affidavit of need than among those whose applications for aid are thoroughly investigated. New York State has been pondering the honor system as a procedure for welfare districts throughout the state. The Ninety-first Congress had on its agenda a bill that proposed a similar approach to welfare assistance for the nation. This bill will now be considered in conjunction with President Nixon's proposal for a complete reorganization of the welfare system. Many whites believe that his plan is a move in the right direction because it establishes a Federal minimum standard for all fifty states. On the other hand, most blacks—and there are whites who share this opinion—object to the $1,600 minimum as being inadequate even for subsistence of a family of four. The National Welfare Rights Committee has quoted $3,200 as a minimum Federal standard for the nation and $5,500 as the minimum for urban areas. A Department of Labor report has upped the latter figure and recommended a $6,000 minimum for urban areas. Basically, the proposal does not bring any significant additional money into the cities where, for the most part, the minimum welfare allowance is already above the $1,600 suggested. Protest has also mounted about the measure requiring mothers of school-age children to accept employment or be cut out of the welfare budget, a step interpreted as coercive in forcing a mother to work, as punitive in denying a mother the right to devote her full energies to bringing up growing children, and as dangerous in further weakening the black family structure. The current hope is that as bills on the proposal are presented, communities will do some very careful homework with the committees involved in drafting the final legislation.

Welfare clients have also talked about the unrealistic clothing allowances, as are, for example, these prices in the New York City welfare budget, the highest in the nation: $4 for a cotton dress; $10 for a "dressy" dress; $7.50 for a man's winter trousers. Instead of these allowances there was for a while an automatic quarterly allowance of $25 per welfare recipient for both clothing and household furnishings. Clients continue to ask for extra allowances because, they say, they have no way of meeting such needs through their own efforts. This is largely true. Over 90 per cent of city welfare money usually goes for aid to dependent children, whose mothers cannot leave them to go out to work, and for assistance to the aged, the blind, and other disabled unemployables. The remaining 10 per cent goes partially as supplementary assistance to heads of households who are working but not earning enough to support their families and to people receiving insufficient unemployment insurance between jobs. An unemployed worker receives approximately half his weekly salary in unemployment insurance benefits; the maximum raised in September 1968 from $55 to $65 per week. But the low-income worker usually earns about $60 per week, netting him $30 in unemployment insurance to support himself and his family. Some of Welfare's 10 per cent goes to employables whose limited basic literacy skills make them, in fact, unemployable.

The welfare picture, however, is still a gloomy one. A closer view reveals that public assistance households include many with no legal father, and in some instances, a mother who says, "I'll have as many children as I want. You can't tell me what to do with

my own body"—a statement which more often reflects a defiance of white authority than any real
desire to bring children who will be public charges
into the world. A number of welfare families are
also hard core cases, third generation recipients who
have never known any other kind of life. Some
critics blame public assistance for perpetuating such
a cycle; others condemn society for not having singled
out young people to offer them educational and vocational opportunities beyond the low expectations of
the ghetto.

At this point, it seems probable that only an adequate living wage for the most unskilled of America's citizens will seriously cope with the problem
of continuing dependency. Most of these unskilled
are Negro men. They are the fathers who try to
balance a minimum $1.60 hourly wage against the
needs of a usually large family— They are also the
legal or putative fathers who abandon their responsibilities when the financial going becomes too rough. If
America expects poor children to grow up into stable,
productive adults, one of its first steps may have to be
to give their fathers the sense of dignity and authority
that the capacity to support a family usually en-
genders. And what else can simultaneously serve to
offer ghetto children a meaningful model with whom
to identify and a chance to develop their own more
positive self–image?

America may balk. Public opinion still rejects the
negative income tax and the guaranteed annual
wage. The concepts are seemingly repugnant to a
society that takes pride in having pulled itself up by
its own bootstraps. A doubling or tripling of the
hourly minimum wage may be a little less difficult

to accept—especially if the Federal government subsidizes, as it may have to, some of the employers involved.

Government is today subsidizing a steadily growing number of earn-as-you-learn programs designed to take the black man out of his public assistance rut or his dead-end job and to teach him marketable skills. The living wage that trainees get while learning is a sore point among many whites. Some view the payments as the only way to allay the frustrations and control the riots; others find them outrageous. That word is interpreted rather cynically by blacks who look back on their whole history in this country as outrageous. But in many cases beneath the cynicism is the wistful thought that grievances about employment—and other issues, too—would be much more easily solved if the white man could ever get himself to care about the ghetto and to do something because he cared.

Black employment grievances are, at this time, complicated by the protests of the poor white man who has his own axe to grind. He definitely resents the current focus on black problems. Even when he has come to grips with his conflicts and decided that hope for him lies in an identification with the poor, regardless of color, he has received comparatively minor satisfaction. He walked, though in small number, with the black man in the 1968 Poor Peoples March and shared with him the mud and the hymns of Resurrection City. But it was the black man's needs, not his, that held the national attention. Unfortunately, as the Reverend Ralph Abernathy quickly stated, there are two Americas in our country today; the blacks who see their problems of poverty aggravated by color and the power structure that reacts in historic terms of black and white. The over-all response to the Poverty March was from a white establishment to the demands of blacks, not those of poor blacks and whites.

There seem to be two Americas involved in the struggle over the education of ghetto children these days, too. Whites who have taken the trouble to discover "the other America" in black ghetto schools agree that society may need to rethink some of its reassuringly familiar pedagogical theories. Certainly something has to be done if black ghetto children are to learn better and to advance with their peers to higher employment. But black and white interests do not always coincide in the suggestions that have been made for solutions.

And there are continuing disorders as the black man persists in telling where it hurts and as a white society slowly responds to his pain. The Urban Coalition, initiated by President Johnson in 1967 and func-tioning since as a national organization with state and city affiliates, involves the country's largest corpora-tions, industries, unions, and community repre-sentation in an effort to identify the Negro problems and to plan for their solution. The Coalition func-tions through task forces assigned to the critical areas of education, economic development, man-power, housing, and health. Chairmen of the task forces include members of industry, labor, and the community.

In New York City, the education task force is sponsoring street-front academies to motivate and train high school dropouts. The task force concen-trating on economic growth has formed three local development corporations which are to establish businesses that will eventually belong to the ghetto. The group concerned with manpower has opened up jobs with promotional opportunities in large corporations and initiated training programs where workers can continue their academic education. The housing group has started to computerize and coordinate data in order to facilitate the planning of ghetto housing contracts, has begun to supply information and technical assistance to local housing development corporations made up of community residents, and is in the process of breaking down the barriers for the apprenticeship of ghetto blacks in housing-related employment—bricklaying, plumbing, carpentry, etc. The health task force is just getting off the ground.

As the white man sees it, such a beginning represents hope. The black man is not so sure. When he punctuates the recitation of his grievances with the bricks and beer bottles that he throws at firemen or with the shooting from ambush at the police, he is expressing, among other emotions, his continuing uncertainty. It is absurd to suppose that whites will accept this terrorism as a basis for desirable social action. They have their own emotions to contend with. One of them is the lingering need to show that they are still the stronger side. There is also the important matter of preserving law and order in their nation. The latter issue is particularly troubling to the black man. America is his country, too—though it must often seem otherwise to him. When, he wonders, will it be sufficiently moved to make unnecessary this preservation of law and order? When will it extend to him his undeniable rights to law and justice?

3.
CADILLACS
AND
BREAD:
The Search
for Status

Like happiness, status has many meanings. For the American Negro, it is often what he considers his psychic income. This represents the emotional satisfaction that he gets when he takes a postal clerk's job on the lowest rung of the Civil Service ladder in preference to better paying work greasing trucks and changing the gas and oil of passing cars. An important difference is involved here. At the post office desk, one dresses like everybody else. As a gas station attendant, one wears a uniform. To the Negro, whose soul cries out for the balm of feeling like other men, the shedding of a uniform can be more meaningful than money.

Status—to the black man—is also a Cadillac with white-wall tires, an out-sized diamond ring that glitters on the small right-hand finger, a $200 gold watch, and all the defiance that underlies this ostentatious display. White society keeps him out of the best neighborhoods, bars him no less subtly from the fashionable resorts, and still does not admit him in any substantial numbers to the nation's prestige jobs. But the establishment cannot prevent him—indeed, it has no such interest—from buying what he pleases. The joy of showing a hostile world that he, a black man, has made it is sometimes worth the cost of the Cadillac.

And status is a feeling of belonging, of emerging out of a history or tradition or culture that offers the sustenance of a proud group identity. In America, the black man has only the history of his slavery to look back on. White supremacy has further advised him that he has nothing to boast about in his African heritage, either. Grass huts were the extent of his achievement in that jungle.

Scholars tell the story rather differently. City democracy seems to have existed in Yoruba on the lower Niger three thousand years before Christ. Pliny describes Ethiopia as a vigorously flourishing country at the time of the Trojan War, when Memnon was its king. Arabian history identifies Bilol, the black man, as friend to Mohammed. The Negroes were among the first to make and use tools, domesticate animals, pursue art, and develop systematic religion. At a time when Europe was still satisfied with stone tools, Africa had invented the art of smelting iron. By the twelfth century, Negroes were exporting iron to India and Java. Sudan in Ethiopia and the Ashantis on the Gold Coast were centers of trade in gold, ivory, wood, forged iron, and works of handicraft. During the Middle Ages, Negro kingdoms in the western Sudan were organized with as high a culture as many of the contemporary states of Europe. Art in the kingdom of Benin was practiced without interruption for centuries. By the sixteenth century, the native brass, bronze, and monumental art surpassed the art in Europe. By the seventeenth century, a literature had developed at Timbuktu, and a university established at San Koro where law, literature, grammar, geography, and surgery were taught.

Religious and tribal wars made possible the rape of the African continent. In the fifteenth century, Africa was spiritually torn by the conflict between Islam and Fetish. Physically, it was a battlefield. The Arabs were coming from the east; the barbarians from the west. The Moors were conquering Egypt. Tribe fought against tribe in a bitter rivalry of conflicting faiths and cultures.

Tribe was also frequently pitted against tribe to facilitate the kidnapping that took place during slave raids. The conscience of the world remained impervious to the black man's pain. To the devout Moslem, he symbolized the hated unconverted. To the fanatic Christian, he represented the sinful heathen. In the liberal spirit of European thought, he was a necessary commodity. The theory of racial inferiority was already being born, for western nations needed labor. Human sympathy was a luxury they could not easily afford.

The current identity of revolutionary blacks with the culture and history of Africa may to a degree be based on knowledge of its past and on some empathy with its present. It is more urgently, however, a reaching out for roots in a time when they were once free and in a land where the white culture has not yet debased the black man.

To white society, this seems a dubious group identity. Whether he feels it or not, the Negro in this country is essentially American. He is perhaps the one ingredient in our mythical melting pot that has actually merged. He may learn—as he is trying to do —to speak Swahili and he may affect a mode of dress that tends to the Yorubian, but his life style remains American. His needs and ambitions are indisputably those of the American urban underclass, removed even from the residual influences of the plantation culture that he or his fathers knew in the South.

But he is also a diminished category in the urban life of America. The inexorable process of perpetuating white superiority has arbitrarily reduced him to the dimensions and character of a dark amorphous mass. He has been denied even a strong sense of personal identity to nourish him.

It is only in the recent past when the features of a Martin Luther King or of a fasting Dick Gregory have been sharply etched in the mass media that the American Negro has materialized as an individual for the white community. In the long years before, he existed largely as an entity that was safely faceless, nameless, and powerless. He was not surprised—as a matter of fact, he often remarked, "To you white people, we all look alike"—when the white man failed to recognize him. He expected to see himself as a composite, or even a caricature, in the white man's literature. And he lived up to the white man's expectations when he remained typically faithful, obedient, and unaspiring.

Most basically, the Negro revolution is a struggle

for status in terms of identity as black Americans. Certain rights go with that status. Certain traditions give way.

The tradition of pleasing the white man definitely goes by the boards. The black revolutionary frowns on the Negro custom of showing his best side to the white community. It is only the passive ghetto Negro who still dresses up when he goes "outside," even if it is just on a downtown shopping expedition. His wife and female children wear blouses and summer dresses so starched that they almost crackle, with gloves and hat, always. The revolutionary black wears his work clothes. He prefers that the white community see him as he is, poor and perhaps dirty, too. If his appearance creates discomfort, so much the better. His status lies in being himself.

The Black Muslims and the extremist revolutionaries, who see more or less eye to eye on many aspects of their struggle for status, seem to split sharply in some of their definitions of the current Negro identity. Both groups are in agreement on such issues as equal employment for black and white, the education of Negro children by black teachers, and the establishment of a separate state or territory where the black man will be maintained by the descendants of his former slavemasters until he is able to provide for himself—a period usually estimated as lasting for twenty-five years. The separation that the Black Muslims are practicing, however, aims to make of the American Negro a figure above the reproach of his white fellow Americans. Black Muslims lead a good life. They do not drink, gamble, take drugs, or dress immodestly. They shun promiscuity and support the family unit. They prohibit intermarriage or race mixing. In their righteousness, they present a proud self–image which they believe the rest of the world has no choice but to respect.

The white world has paid them scant attention. Malcolm X, their most outspoken leader, preached hatred and separatism before his visit to Mohammed, the Prophet, in Jerusalem. Upon his return from Mecca, he talked of the brotherhood of man. The movement is splintered now that he is dead. Elijah Muhammed, national spiritual leader of the Muslims, who administers and guides his movement from national headquarters in Chicago, still believes in strict separation.

The rest of the black world finds the rigors of the Muslim life too demanding. But its basic rejection is on philosophic grounds. Today's ghetto black does not want to be any better than the white man. He is tired of all that wasted effort. He wants to be like the white man, good, bad, or in between, and accepted as such by the white community.

The extremist black revolutionary goes still farther. He flaunts his indifference to what the white man thinks of him. His deliberate vulgarity often becomes almost ritualtistic. In an inverse sense, it is as obviously guarded as the placation by the Negro moderate or the disciplined self–expectations of the dedicated Muslim.

What the revolutionary black is largely substituting for his efforts to please the white man—and for his defensiveness about his imperfections—is his pride in his blackness. He is challenging the white world's assumptions that white is superior to black. He is threatening the white world's values by believing that the black man can do everything that the white man can. In his aspirations for status, he is also insisting that the power structure provide him with services which interest the black, rather than the dominant white community, and that it meet his demands if only because he, a black man, has made them.

The addition of Swahili to the curriculum of a Bronx high school is an example of black pressure for a service which the white community stated was both unnecessary and difficult to provide. It was actually only after considerable searching that a person eligible to teach the language was located. Seventeen students registered for the course the first year it was given; twelve, the second. But classes for sixty have since been organized in a junior high school. It is difficult to state with any certainty whether this curriculum innovation is a result of black community pressure or an indication that black adolescents find the cultural identification meaningful enough to overcome their usual resistance to the study of "useless" foreign languages.

The struggle extends, of course, beyond the schools —though education is believed by many black parents today to be perhaps the most important way out of the ghetto trap for their children. As even some sympathetic white liberals see it, the black revolutionary is now proposing to replace the inequities that he has suffered with injustices which he is about to perpetrate on others. He is recommending quotas for employment and for university admission—a practice that the white liberal has just finished congratulating himself on having abolished. Because the Negro represents eleven per cent of the American population and the Jew less than three per cent, this move is sometimes interpreted as at least faintly anti-Semitic. The black revolutionary is also voicing his less than complete satisfaction with the merit system in Civil Service, the implication being that he would not be averse to the favors of political patronage, provided he were the beneficiary. But the white liberal is proud of the progress made in destroying the power of the political bosses and has no intention of supporting reactionary regression. The Negro revolutionary is demanding far greater representation in professional and technical occupations. But the proportion of Negroes in such fields in New York City, at least, is already higher than that of the Irish or Italians and the reactions are naturally hostile.

Negroes may object that these comparisons are not really equitable. In their opinion, the basis of measurement should be the number of total blacks versus the number of all whites, not versus one or another section of the white population.

Negroes may also admit that some of their proposals are perhaps not completely fair to other entrenched or aspiring minorities. The concern is not very deep, however. White America has rarely been entirely fair to Negroes. And in this transitional period of the black revolution, when most Negroes are still unable to compete on equal terms with more advantaged whites, quota representation—and political favor, too—are frankly accepted as a means to an end.

The revolutionary black has definitely made his

decision. In the interests of his self–assertion—and of the status and power that self–assertion imply—he has cast off his tradition of placating the white man. He has, moreover, developed the strength to disagree with him.

The younger black generation, particularly in urban areas, has seemingly also given up the traditional Negro dependence on the solace of religion. The white man—if only because he played such an active role in developing that tradition—must surely find this displeasing, too.

It was the white man who originally introduced the Negroes to Christianity. Truly religious whites may have been thinking of the advancement of the City of God on earth or hoping to secure points for themselves in heaven when they spread the Christian gospel. But the conversion of the black man was more generally undertaken for reasons which had little or nothing to do with the spirit of Christ's teachings. A firm belief in that promised land with "no sickness, no toil, no danger" that lay "over Jordan" could help discourage Negro rebellion. A black man could endure and wait if he knew that one day he would ride "the glory train" to his home of deliverance in heaven. During the more than four hundred years of American slavery, the church was the only unifying force the white man permitted the Negro. In the years since, the church has remained about the only American institution the Negro could enter freely, as long as he stayed on his side of the tracks.

The church is still today an important part of the religious and social life of the rural and ghetto Negro. It may even be that the young urban extremist who exhorts his friends to violence on weekdays goes to church regularly on a Sunday. His rhetoric is what makes him seem so irreligious.

But for him—and for many Negroes—the meaning of religion appears to be changing. A sense of mission is replacing the resignation. God must surely want justice for the black man, as well as for the white. Ralph Abernathy, devout minister of the church, has said that it is God, not Lester Maddox or George Wallace who rules in the South. And Ralph Abernathy has not told his people to be humble and submissive. He has led them, as Martin Luther King, another minister of the church, intended, on their militant poverty march. Their protest is, in a way, a religious crusade.

Most American Negroes, educated in schools where Negro history is not taught or where the teaching has been limited to a listing of revered black baseball players, jazz musicians, or prizefighters, know little of their background of protest. It cost the lives of sixty million African Negroes to bring ten million slaves to America. Rebellion in this country broke out as early as 1522, on a sugar plantation. In 1527, there was an uprising in Florida. Insurrections took place in Virginia in 1710, in New York in 1712, South Carolina in 1713, Boston in 1723, Rhode Island and Massachusetts in 1730, Georgia in 1816. Denmark Vesey, a free Negro, organized revolt in South Carolina in 1822. The famous Nat Turner Rebellion took place in Virginia in 1831. Then the Emancipation Proclamation came along to lull the Negro into an illusion of equality. That lasted for more than a century.

These days, the black man is writing his own proclamation. It spells out his worth as an individual and grants him the opportunity to make a contribution to his world. In a larger sense, this is an emancipation for all of contemporary society. It accords to even the "lowliest" the status of a man among men.

4.
WE
WANT
IN:
The Changing
Black Organizations

The revolt of the young Turks from the National Association for the Advancement of Colored People (NAACP) in 1968—not the first such action, incidentally—is undoubtedly symbolic of a trend in Negro insurgency today. Essentially, the young people levelled two accusations at the venerable Association: remoteness from the grassroots elements of the Negro population and an over–polite attitude in relation to the white establishment. Both reflect the current Negro impatience with the slow rate of change. Whether this takes the form of a return to Africa movement or is expressed in the dream of black and white within the American structure someday walking hand in hand, the underlying purpose appears to be the same. In a world of expanding freedoms and opportunities, the American Negro wants *in* and he wants it during his lifetime.

A resultant fluidity seems to mark the character

of most Negro organizations. Some, of course, are more quick to change than others. The N.A.A.C.P., as by far the oldest and most traditional of the civil rights movements, (it started in 1909), preserves a measured pace. It remains a biracial organization, depending for change on the normal democratic processes. It achieves its objectives through legislation for social action projects in such fields as job opportunity, education, housing, etc., through judicial rulings on test cases in local and higher courts, and through the work of its defense league which provides legal council on civil rights issues, even in the deep South. At this point in history, the N.A.A.C.P. is caught between the white obstructionists who feel that the Negro has been given too many concessions already and the black power groups that place little faith in procedures which involve the cooperation of the white man. The vote at the 1968 convention in Atlantic City, New Jersey, was for a continuation of the usual N.A.A.C.P. approach with a greater emphasis on the program of social action projects. Approximately one thousand young Turks walked out of the convention in protest, however. If the growing demand for direct local action is any indication, their numbers will probably swell by the next meeting. The old order may not completely give way to the new, but the chances are good that as senior members and officers retire from active participation, the posture of the N.A.A.C.P. will yield in response to the pressures of the young.

The National Urban League, another traditional organization, is beginning to show subtle signs of change. Basically, it is a service agency, biracial in character, and concentrating on projects designed both to improve the skills of Negroes and to open up job opportunities for them. Since its inception in 1910, the Urban League has worked largely with foundations and industries for the attainment of its goals. Through the years, it has been singularly successful in placing eligible Negroes in management and executive positions. It has moved closer to the grassroots recently with its Street Academies, the storefront schools that are intended to attract the high school dropout. A carefully planned program hopefully provides the student with educational remediation and an incentive to return to high school and, again hopefully, with the desire to go on to college. The Urban League has also made a great point of preferential job treatment for the Negro to bridge the social, economic, and educational gap that separates him from his fellow Americans. And its Operation Open City, started in 1964, is now concentrating on integrated housing. Here, the Urban League works to implement fair housing laws, wherever these exist, and to educate communities through meetings with landlords and with tenant groups to a greater receptivity toward mixed housing patterns. Most important of all, perhaps, is the growing sensitivity by the Urban League to the rumblings of what Whitney Young, its executive director, describes as the "storm that will surely engulf all of us if tangible, meaningful results are not achieved with speed and sincerity." Mr. Young, too, endorses black power —he stated this publicly in the summer of 1968—but only in terms of responsible Negro political and economic strength to attain the results that would make unnecessary a storm of hate and despair.

The dramatic changes in the organization and philosophy of the Congress of Racial Equality (CORE) and of the Student Non-violent Coordinating Committee (SNCC) are interpreted by some as the signals of the impending storm. Both are dominated by a membership which discourages white participation and feels nothing but scepticism about either the white man's empathy for the lot of the Negro or his intention of offering—or going along with—any programs of genuine meaning for the black man. The anti-white ideology seems to preclude any use of the traditional channels of change and to focus largely on a hostile black and white confrontation.

CORE, organized in 1942 as a biracial group with a large white membership, stressed from the beginning a grassroots base. Its goals were equal opportunities for Negroes in employment, education and housing, in the use of public accommodations, and in the area of voter registration. As more militant black nationalists joined CORE ranks, the cry rose for an organization with a black identity, that is, for an organization with black leadership and in which decisions would be made exclusively by blacks. Between 1963 and 1964, CORE lost most of its white membership. By 1965, when James Farmer resigned as its director, a number of CORE chapters had begun to move in a separatist direction. Under Floyd McKissick, its new director, several CORE chapters pursued the policy of working for a separate black state, one of them purchasing, it is believed, property in North Carolina for Negroes to develop their own political and economic system. Roy Innis, who replaced Mr. McKissick as acting director in 1968, enunciated the CORE purpose as a restructuring

of the American nation into two autonomous societies. The black society, according to Mr. Innis, will
eventually have complete control over the institutions
that deliver goods and services to the black communities. This includes police, fire, and sanitation
departments. CORE opposes the recommended decentralized school system in New York City. It prefers that Harlem own its own schools. The money for
all of this, as CORE envisions it, is to come from the
taxes paid by Negroes—not an eminently practical
idea at this time when so many Negroes in urban
areas are earning too little to pay taxes; but perhaps
CORE is looking forward to higher wages under its
own economic system. At any rate, the organization
rejects all other programs as "Mickey Mouse" projects
which serve only to postpone what Innis calls "the
eventual crisis." And without an enormous domestic
effort, Mr. Innis believes the crisis will materialize
as the only viable channel for the Negro who wants
in.

The Student Non-violent Coordinating Committee,
beginning, as its name implies, as an organization
oriented to non-violence, represents perhaps an even
more revolutionary trend. It emerged in 1960 out of
an impetus by idealistic college students—black and
white—to do something to help the Negro in the
South. Their chief area of work was the mobilization
of political forces where the Negro had the balance
of power in terms of numbers. They started with
voter registration. Groups of young field workers,
Stokely Carmichael among them, went into the deep
South to explain the importance of the vote and to
organize voter registration in states where Negroes

were being deprived of their legal right to vote. The means by which Southern communities kept Negroes out of the polling booths varied. They included physical intimidation (there are still lynchings in Mississippi), economic boycotts through threats of job loss or of discontinued patronage of small businesses —such as the laundry many Negro women did in their homes for white families—a poll tax which a dominant white community made certain the average Negro citizen could not afford to pay, and literacy tests which required him to read, depending on the state, either from the United States Constitution or from the constitution of a particular state. The poll tax was, by 1964, abolished in all but five of the Southern states; the Twenty-fourth Amendment to the Constitution, which became law in 1964, has forbidden the payment of a poll tax as a requirement for voting in any state. The literacy tests were suspended by the 1965 Civil Rights law, which also permitted Federal examiners to register voters where anti-Negro bias by local registrars seemed to make this necessary. The work of the dedicated young S.N.C.C. volunteers and the resultant exposé of voting conditions in the South undoubtedly contributed to these changes.

S.N.C.C. workers carried no weapons when they went into the states of North Carolina, Mississippi, and Alabama. They launched no campaigns of hate. Negro suffrage was their one crusade. But many of them were attacked and beaten by Southern whites. Three—James Chaney, a Negro from Mississippi, and Andrew Goodman and Michael Schwerner, white, from New York—were shot to death. Carmichael's

own conversion to aggressiveness against the white
man may have started when he was tear-gassed several
times during the early days of S.N.C.C. It was apparently then that he embraced the racist black
power that he has espoused ever since.

When he became S.N.C.C. chairman in 1966,
Carmichael stated that he was not ready to start any
violent actions against whites but that he would be
prepared at all times to strike back. It seems to be in
this spirit that he adopted "black power" as the
S.N.C.C. slogan. It quickly became the national Negro
battle cry.

The tactics of the street that Mr. Carmichael has
since openly applauded are evidently interpreted by
him and by S.N.C.C. followers as the black man's
striking back. Retaliation in this context is not necessarily confined to actions stimulated by violence
visited on the Negro. S.N.C.C. members can strike
back against social injustice, economic restriction, or
even an educational system. They, it has been maintained, pushed their black power ideology in the disputes between the decentralized school units and the
New York City Board of Education.

As a movement committed to black arrogant racism
and, if need be, to quick violence for the purpose of
opening up channels of opportunity for the black
man, S.N.C.C. has an enormous appeal for the young.
Stokley Carmichael's move toward extreme militancy
was followed by an even more aggressive leadership
when H. Rap Brown became S.N.C.C. chairman in
1967. Mr. Brown has since been jailed for carrying a
gun across a state border. For him, this may have been
the act of preparation in the S.N.C.C. striking–back

policy. For the United States government, it was an opportunity to put behind bars—temporarily, at least—an advocate of violence and disorder. The new S.N.C.C. chairman seems to be more soft-spoken, less inclined to threats and incitement. In his opening speech, he stressed self-help programs, such as effective community organization and the establishment of black-owned businesses, to help change the character of the nation's ghettos.

The Black Panthers, organized in Los Angeles in 1966, share with S.N.C.C. the concept of fighting back. Their membership in the Bay area is minimal, probably one hundred and fifty to two hundred. But Black Panthers are both verbal and active and it is suspected that their national ranks are growing. Their menacing uniforms have been seen in city after city and their call for an end to the treatment of blacks as a "colonized people" has been used as a springboard by militant extremists across the country. They have been arming themselves to be ready to "retaliate," particularly against the police brutality that they anticipate will come as a reaction to Negro rioting. They would like to make these riots much more organized than they have been. They have also spurred the development of a black political party, to be activated by recruitment on a house-to-house basis.

All of these organizations want *in* for the black man. The Southern Christian Leadership Conference wants *in* for all of the poor and downtrodden. The press coverage after Dr. King's death reminded those who needed reminding that it was Rosa Parks, the Negro seamstress with the tired feet, who indirectly started the

S.C.L.C. Her arrest, after she refused to go to the back of the bus, sparked the Montgomery, Alabama bus boycott and brought Dr. King from his pulpit to lead the "Stride toward Freedom." When the United States Supreme Court declared the Alabama segregation laws unconstitutional in 1956, Dr. King's house was bombed. But the S.C.L.C., representing religious leaders from ten states, went on to protest against discrimination in transportation, in restaurant service, and in the use of public accommodations in the South. Dr. King's militant non-violence was hardly passive resistance. It was civil disobedience of unjust segregation laws and direct confrontation with authorities over the changing of such laws. Sit-ins, lie-ins, pray-ins, mass marches in the streets, and the almost certain risk of being beaten and jailed were all part of it.

Dr. King marched first for laws to establish equality. When he brought his 1963 Civil Rights March on Washington to its climactic close, he said to the 200,000 people who were standing with him in the shadow of the Lincoln Memorial, and to the millions more who were watching on television, "I have a dream." He said it again and again, each time measuring out the distance between "the American dream" and the reality of being a black man in America. And he went on with his struggle to make the American dream part of every man's heritage.

He marched then for equal economic opportunities. He called for a Bill of Rights for the disadvantaged, both black and white, one that would provide adequately "for the least of God's children, here and around the world."

He moved from the local to the national and then

to the international scene. He expressed his opinion on Vietnam for which some Americans condemned him and others, who believed that domestic and foreign non-violence should not be paired, called him foolish.

There are those who say that if he had lived, Dr. King might have helped to reconcile the two societies, one white and one black, which in the opinion of the President's "Riot Commission," seem to be developing in the United States. It is true that some black power youth referred to him derisively as De Lawd. But the great mass of Negroes across the country called him their Moses and trusted him to lead them out of their desert. And the white power structure, if it ever reached the point of wanting to hear a black man out, might have chosen Dr. King, winner of the Nobel Peace prize in 1964, to listen to. He, at least, continued to talk the language of domestic peace.

But there are many who contend that Dr. King was beginning to lose his credibility with the black people. His efforts caused Congress to pass in 1964 the most far-reaching civil rights bill this country has ever had. And in 1965, after the King-led march from Selma to Montgomery, Congress passed the much-hoped for Voting Rights Act. But neither of these measures materially improved the living conditions of the average Negro. The civil rights legislation did not move him out of segregated housing. The opportunities for wider suffrage did not result in laws to create more jobs or better medical care or improved welfare services. On the contrary, funds for anti-poverty programs were being cut nationally. Dr. King, his detractors say, would have had to take a harder line with the white establishment if he was to get it to deliver to the poor Negro—and to the poor white. His own organization, they maintain, would have fallen apart if he didn't.

Dr. King might indeed have exerted more pressure. He spoke of the need for Negroes to learn how to organize their strength into compelling power so that the government could not elude their demands. But it is doubtful that strength meant violence to him. He was working, as he so often said, for a positive peace. He hoped for the presence of justice in this land, not for a negative absence of tension. He hoped even to reach the angriest of the rioters and make them "disciplined legions for sound goals."

Some of the more extremist groups may be giving serious thought to such considerations. When the Kansas City, Philadelphia, Bronx, and Brooklyn chapters stalked out of the CORE national convention in July 1968, it was in protest against the moderation of the national organization. They accused the national leadership of having done little or nothing for the black people in the last year and a half and of having caused the organization and its program to lose all meaning for the local communities. (The condemnation was not directed at Innis, who had only recently been appointed acting director.) But no significant change in national policy emerged in response to these charges. The dissension may at this time represent in-fighting for organizational position. It may also be that a more basic split is developing over the ideological question of whether to establish the national movement as entirely separatist or to consider a structural policy of working for change within the existing system.

The new S.N.C.C. leadership may well be pondering the same issues. In August 1968, S.N.C.C. and Stokely Carmichael parted company by mutual consent, presumably because his views were not in keeping with the new thinking. Recent developments show a swing in the direction of organizing S.N.C.C. as a political party. A black panther has been chosen for its emblem which probably means that the Black Panthers are also involved in the effort. As a political party, S.N.C.C. and the Black Panther movement will apparently be working for change within the established structure.

There are no absolutes about the black revolution. There is only the fact that extremists and moderate militants are fighting for the same essential cause. Both, in their way, have moved a white America to some awareness of the black man's need for status and opportunity and involvement in his own destiny. Both now face the hard-core issues of open housing and compensatory economic opportunity and the political role of the Negro in his own inner city and in American society as a whole. Whether these battles will be waged by all blacks versus all whites or by blacks with the support of some whites against the remnants of an intransigent white establishment is yet to be determined. Isolation was the choice of certain blacks largely as a response to what seemed a totality of white opposition and to the continued tendency of the white man to try to make the black man's decisions for him.

By now, these separatists have made their self—assertion abundantly clear. And in their more practical moments, when rage and the intoxicating illusion of power do not completely take over, they must surely consider the futility, for both blacks and whites, of a divisive revolution. What will probably come instead is a series of smaller confrontations, each one over a specific issue; each, possibly, pushing to the breaking point the patience and good will of its combatants.

5.
HELP
YOURSELF
LIKE WE DID:
Jobs and Job
Qualifications
for Blacks

Whatever else the Negro Revolution achieves, it has succeeded in exposing the multiple pathology of the black-white controversy. The symptoms are bitterly acted out in the arguments and resentments about jobs and job qualifications.

It is probably fair to say that the average white American is rather taken aback by the kind of employment demands the militant Negroes are making. Even the white liberal reacts with some feeling of bafflement when the unskilled or semi-skilled Negro appears less than eager to accept a "good" job as bus boy or porter or building superintendent. When the rhetoric of Bayard Rustin, perhaps the mildest of the revolutionaries, advises that pushing a cart in the garment district is un-American, the bafflement is more than likely to turn to fury.

The white man is understandably responding out of his own experiential or familial background. Didn't his father or grandfather or other remote ancestor start out in this country on the bottom of the social and economic ladder? Wasn't this impoverished immigrant able to pull himself up from ditch digger or sweatshop worker or sidewalk peddler by his own efforts? Didn't he so live that his son became a doctor; his daughter, a teacher; and his grandson, an atom scientist? And aren't they all residing in fashionable suburbia with a car available to every adult and adolescent member of the family and television or stereo sets all around them? "Why don't you help yourself like we did?" the white man asks now, his voice harsh with the near or dim memory of the struggle.

Immersed thus in his nostalgia, he may neglect to observe a historical difference in the legacy of the American Negro. The Afro-American knows no precedent for upward mobility. During the five generations that the period since emancipation encompasses, only a comparative handful of his people have made it up from that bottom rung on the ladder. For the vast majority, there is no heritage of hope and strength and fulfillment.

From the camp of the white extremists, the answers come quickly. The Negro is primitive, shiftless, involved with the moment, unmindful of the future, periodically drunk, and obsessed with sex. More inquiring minds seek deeper understanding, explanations that may also account for the supposed heedlessness, improvidence, and orgies, primitive or otherwise. Some of the explanations are not very difficult to find. They are part of our American tradition.

The plantation owner probably defined the tradition

originally when he said, "Our slaves have good homes and plenty to eat. When they are sick, we take good care of them." The slaves are legally free now. But the white man is still taking care of the Negroes. He is taking such good care of them that he cannot even allow them the heroism of trying to do something for themselves and failing.

It is a complex process, this "taking care" of the American Negro. It involves the white man in finding a job for him—as bellboy, porter, handyman, garbage man, janitor, or shoe-shine boy, with "a chance for good tips" in the white man's barber shop. It does not involve the white man in thinking about training that shoe-shine boy, however skilled and reliable he may be, to become a barber in his shop. It does require of the white man a certain degree of tolerance, preferably the amused kind, when the handyman/bellboy/shoe-shine boy et al admits that he spent his wages and applies for a small loan. And it expects the black man to say, as he often has, "I work for a good boss man. Any time I want a $5 or $10 loan, he gives it to me."

It is a process in which certain roles are made to emerge. The Negro is the perpetual child; the white man, the benevolent—but ever-controlling—parent. Growth is not encouraged. The white employer contrives, consciously or unconsciously, to communicate the idea that he is doing the Negro a favor in hiring him and in keeping him on the job. It rarely occurs to the white man to think of the Negro as a worker who might have a contribution to make. After a while, the idea will occur to the Negro less and less frequently, too. He will learn, instead, to know his place. He will learn to smile when the white man calls him, by now a grandfather, "boy." He will learn to please the white man, to placate him, and to turn his anger inward to hate himself. And he will stay on that bottom rung of the employment ladder on this job—or on another, if in a mood of despair, drunk or sober, he calls the first one quits. He will stay there because he is fighting a losing battle with history and tradition and there is nowhere he can go to make things better.

Perhaps it would be more relevant to see the employer-employe relationship in terms of master and slave. In this context, the lack of upward mobility becomes even clearer. Today, more than one hundred years after liberation, the Negro is totally dependent on the white economic structure for his existence. He owns no big banks, no large factories, no nation-wide corporations. He merits no substantial credit extensions to make possible such ownership. Perhaps even more significant, he plays little or no part in the decision-making that rules his life. It is only in the last ten years—and principally because of the civil rights furor—that Negroes have sat on boards which determine policies about wages and unions and housing and welfare and book learning and have made their recommendations for the upward economic mobility of the black man. Such opportunities are still noticeably scarce.

Educators are fond of saying that the Negro would get places the same as the white man if he had more interest in schooling. But educators also consider motivation of primary importance in the learning situation. In the life of the American Negro, this educationally compelling factor is largely missing.

It may indeed be unrealistic to expect such motivation. The place that history and tradition have marked out for the American Negro requires little aspiration. The role of a life-long placating child calls for a different kind of education than is provided in the usual school curriculum. Most schools place high on their priority lists the American dream of *From Log Cabin to the White House.* Only by the implications of omission, do they teach the place of the American Negro. They are also inclined to be somewhat cagey about "telling it like it is" where actual restrictions on Negro efforts to better themselves are concerned.

To what degree these restrictions on upward mobility are calculated or unthinking may perhaps be argued. Either way, however, they add up to an impressive list: The quality of Southern education is for the most part so poor that college graduates usually need a refresher course in spelling and sentence construction before they can apply for a civil service job. The Southern Negro high school usually offers a curriculum so limited that graduates do not have a chance even to be exposed to the subjects required for admission by the local state university. Industry hires token Negroes for the sake of a good public image. Industry usually proceeds to relegate token and other Negro employes to jobs on the lowest performance levels. Father and son unions automatically—since most white fathers have no black sons—exclude Negroes forever. Many unions have entrance examinations. These are required of Negroes only; whites may serve an apprenticeship. One examination, passed by all sixteen Negro applicants, was immediately declared invalid by the union; the courts subsequently reversed the decision. Difficulties are still put in the way of suffrage, making it impractical for many Negroes to exercise their legal right to vote. If a Negro candidate is elected, the white community will know who voted for him. Economic pressure can go to work quickly. A Negro who wants his job does not disturb the political scene.

No, the Negro is definitely not motivated to learn, to improve, to "help himself like we did." How can he, with such lack of expectation? Such a minimum sense of accomplishment? Such a feeling of rejection from the larger America?

But some Negroes have made it. More and more are working in middle–class jobs, even in administrative positions, in government, industry, and business. These are the "different" Negroes, as the white man puts it.

They are indeed different. They have probably never known the self-image of being "nothin'." They may not have been taught at their mother's knee that aggressive competitiveness is painfully unacceptable in the outside white society. They may not have lived in a home where the daily challenge was for physical survival, not for higher horizons. The tag of un-educable was perhaps not so consistently applied to them by middle–class white—or black—teachers. Nor were they, perhaps, quite so casually directed by the school guidance counselor—because they were black and "what else can they be expected to do?"—to the higher education of manual skills courses. In one way or another, their experiences were not the usual lot of the Negro. And they were able to develop the strength to compete, to fight, to assert themselves. But their numbers are few—almost as few as the Germans who defied Hitler or the Russians who talked back to Stalin. What made them tick?

The black revolution is not particularly concerned with these "different" fortunate souls. It is concentrating on the black masses. And to them, it is extending a heady brew.

Economically, it is offering them the expectations of of an affluent white America. The image of Sambo servility is totally excluded from this prospect. Indeed, it is precisely because of their service nature that the black revolutionary today spurns the jobs of waiter, attendant, delivery boy, and such. If he is to move onward and upward with the rest of America, he must tread warily. He dare not let himself be caught up in anything even remotely remindful of a former state of servitude.

Ah! The white community listens. And its own rhetoric goes into action. The rebuttal runs something like this: Slavery is as old as man. The Egyptians enslaved the Jews; the Romans, the Greeks; the Saracens, the Christians. Slavery was actually a condition of war. Whole nations were enslaved. But they got over it. They were not too lazy to work hard. They did not expect things to be handed to them. And most certainly, they did not display the arrogance of a Stokely Carmichael or a Daniel Watts or an H. Rap Brown.

The black revolutionary hardly bothers to counter such forays into historical analogy. If he did, he might say that there are gradations even in slavery, that the American institution was unique in its destruction of the Negro family, its disregard of individual human affections, and its treatment of the

Negro genus man as chattel. He might add two other thoughts. The first is that Lincoln's eloquent proclamation is more highly revered as a yellowing piece of copybook paper than as a national way of life. The second is that the arrogance of the black militant leaders is the quality that most endears them to their followers. For them, the arrogance is a symbol of all their rage and frustration and impotence at last turned outward and aggressively directed at the white man, any white man.

The black revolutionary makes his demands in this very climate of incendiarism. Unfortunately, it is only when the white man is able to combine both mind and heart in an empathetic effort to "think Negro" that he can see these demands as the black man's ways of helping himself. Most whites do not know this insight. The black way is too unfamiliar, too removed from their own diligent, step-by-step, goal-oriented progress.

The black revolutionary wants *in* for his people on all levels of economic society. He wants instant *in*. Necessarily, he has his own special standards for getting in and staying there.

If a Negro applicant for a clerical or managerial job does not write acceptable English, he is not to be rejected. He is to be hired and trained to do better while he is on the job. If a Negro employe does not report to work regularly, and when he does, is habitually late, he is not to be discharged, perhaps not even reprimanded. His work patterns are to be tolerated while he is gradually helped to learn and to accommodate himself to required job disciplines. If he is hostile to fellow employes and irresponsible about job duties, this is to be understood, too, in the light of his history, his very vulnerable ego, and his continuing need for positive reassurances. The inability of large numbers of Negro high school graduates to make the grades for college admission is to be handled with similar flexibility—through the lowering of college entrance requirements or through the provision, by the college, of special compensatory programs to bring applicants up to par.

Such adjustments, laudatory as they may be in principle, demand of the white man a revolution in his own carefully structured set of values. He can hardly be expected to accept the threat with any great ease or grace. Even some black men experience qualms about the differing standards. They smack too much of traditional paternalism, in the first place. In the second, they veer dangerously in the direction of separatism, a condition which the integrationist Negro views as definitely retrogressive in a democratic society. They serve only to compound his problem.

For the white man, the issues are simpler. He may yield to the demands for a number of reasons: the world is changing; nothing is what it used to be; there is, possibly, another way of looking at things; and most important, that other way represents, today, the popular, liberal position. The white man rarely yields, however, in direct response to Negro militancy. Then, to the white man, adaptation looks too much like capitulation. Then, an imminent reversal of traditional Negro and white roles looms ominously. Then, the white man cries *never* to the black revolutionary shouts of *now*.

The battle becomes even more shrill when the

revolutionary Negro moves on to the next step of his self-help program, the part that he refers to as controlling his own destiny. In the pursuit of this effort, he has lately been concentrating on the education of his young, an occupation seemingly eminently in keeping with white traditions of upward mobility. Actually, it is one of the most controversial items on the revolutionary agenda—partly because of the visibility of black power in action and partly because of black power excesses.

Negro-dominated local school boards are currently controlling curriculum and personnel in a number of ghetto schools. It is probably true that, in their inexperience, they are making some foolish mistakes. They are urging the teaching of black culture when there is probably no culture—except, ironically enough, American—that is common to United States blacks. Some are clamoring for the teaching of Swahili which is not even a native African tongue but a kind of pidgin language developed by Arab traders. Ironically, again, it was the Arab traders who initiated the practice of capturing African blacks for export as slaves— a historical footnote that creeps unbidden into the cherished amicable Arab-Black Power relationships.

At this point in American history, control by the Negro of his destiny may well mean, if the extremist revolutionaries are to have their way, an existence of self-imposed educational apartheid for the black person. It is a shocking thought to the onlooker, particularly to the hopeful liberal, looking forward— perhaps in theory only—to housing relocation which would make de facto school segregation a distant memory, in the future. To the black man caught up in the exhilaration of a freedom he has never really known, only the present may matter.

Part of the freedom involves the luxury of being able to make a mistake. Not all Negroes engaged in the black school effort are completely sure that they are doing the right thing. But they are quick to tell the white man he has not always been perfect, either. He did not teach the Negro child to read. He did not sufficiently help the Negro youth to overcome the inhibiting environment of the ghetto so that he could stay in school and make something of himself. "Why, from us," they ask, "do you expect instant success?"

The question is perceptive. To answer it, the white man must face the complexity of his own anxieties. He has exhorted the Negro to "help yourself like we did." But the Negro self-help revolution has both outraged and unnerved him. It has been too fast, too frenzied, too disposed to easy violence. The pure and obdurate hatred of the white man that it has exposed has robbed him of even the charity of his understanding. He cannot allow the militants the pathos of their bombast. He cannot see the strength in their awkwardness. He cannot wish them well in undertakings which augment their brashness and raise their hopes of power. Power can be synonymous with tyranny. And the white man, like Nat Turner, may be remembering his Isaiah, "Therefore will I number you to the sword, and ye shall all bow down to the slaughter: because when I called ye did not answer."

6.
EQUAL
OPPORTUNITY
OR
EQUAL RIGHTS?

In a nation committed by legal decree and boastful tradition to the ideal of human equality, the Negro clamor for equal rights must certainly have come as a considerable shock. It probably began with the dismayed acceptance of the need for civil rights legislation. Despite the guarantees of our Declaration of Independence and of three Civil War period amendments which reassert the equality of all American citizens, action was urged and taken to legalize the rights of the black man. Specific laws now give him a number of heretofore largely unknown privileges. He can—theoretically, at least—learn his three R's and pursue his higher education in a non-segregated school, present his qualifications for a job for which he thinks he is eligible, sit alongside a white man at a lunch counter, ride in an undesignated space in a bus; and make freer use of the public parks, swimming pools, and toilet facilities of our country. He has not yet won the complete battle for open housing but he expects, depending on his point of view, that a crisis of conscience on the part of the white man or riots in the streets by angry blacks, will ultimately yield some victory here, too. And he has extended his emancipation struggle to another plane, that of equality of opportunity.

The concept of equality of opportunity goes beyond the acquisition of equal rights. Equality of opportunity is what Whitney Young calls the special effort that will make it possible for Negroes to take advantage of their equal rights. Threatened whites and less cautious blacks more bluntly call it preferential treatment for the Negro. Some refer to it as "a piece of the action."

The push toward equal opportunity grows out of the admission by Negro revolutionaries and conservatives alike that the black man is unable to compete in today's highly complex society. In a sense, it is a historic inevitability. More than three centuries of keeping the American Negro in his place have effectively served their purpose. By and large, the American Negro is now unable, without help, to get out of that place. The granting of equal rights does not automatically provide him with the poise, the confidence, the education, and the skills he needs to enter the competition on approximately equal terms. It does not, in many cases, even stir him out of his apathetic unwillingness to compete at all.

There can be no apology for the enslavement—literal or subtle—of one race by another. There can only be attempts at redemption. A still shaky alliance between blacks of moderately militant persuasion and whites involved in the power structure is currently working out a program to make equal opportunity a reality for the Negro. But the attendant babble of protests, from the embittered backlash on the one hand and from the apostles of black power on the other, is disturbingly reminiscent of Genesis: "Come, let us go down, and there confuse their language that they may not understand one another's speech."

Removed from these complexly motivated disparities, the program seems sensible enough. It provides career ladder opportunities for Negroes serving in what are termed paraprofessional positions in city agencies, compensatory education for college-bound black youth, and on-the-job training contracts with private industry. It is hoped that the program will expand into the field of local economic development to help reduce poverty in ghetto areas.

Career ladder opportunities expose the Negro to professional environments while motivating and encouraging him to improve himself. The Nelson-Scheuer Act, passed by Congress in 1967, now called the Public Services Careers Act, provides Federal funds for the salaries of non-high school graduates (in actuality, largely Negro), to be hired by city agencies, and for the referral of these employes to free high school equivalency classes. Receipt of a high school equivalency diploma entitles an employe to move a step higher on his job. The diploma also establishes his eligibility for admission to day or evening classes in a free two-year community college. Graduation leads to promotion to a still higher job step and eligibility for transfer to a city university offering a B.A. or a B.S. degree. It is expected that the simultaneous work-study experience will enrich and make more meaningful both the job performance and the related college courses.

Implementation of the Nelson-Scheuer Act so far has proven fairly simple. In a number of large cities, non-high school graduates are entering the fields of education, health, welfare, recreation, and library services as aides to be promoted as they go on with their education to positions as assistants and, ultimately, as professionals. They are relieving harassed professionals of some of their burdensome physical and clerical responsibilities—escorting small children to and from a lunchroom, for example, or filling the orange juice glasses on a hospital tray, or making out a library card. And they are being promptly registered in the rapidly expanding high school equivalency classes. At the moment, the chance for upward mobility seems particularly significant in the health services where the lowest paid and most demeaning jobs—those of nurses' aides, attendants, and orderlies —are identified with Negroes and Puerto Ricans. It may eventually prove even more important in the welfare field. The Welfare Department in New York City has invited public assistance recipients to work as welfare aides while they are exposed to the education they need to become social investigators.

The section of the Equal Opportunity program dealing with compensatory education offers positive hope and action to young black people. Both public and private colleges admit promising young Negroes who, for various environmental reasons, have not prepared themselves for college entrance. Some colleges admit high school students during the summer ending their junior year to help acclimate them to the mores of a college campus. These colleges may follow the students' progress during their senior high school year to offer necessary guidance and at the close of the senior year again admit them to a summer experience on campus. The New York City Human Resources Administration has gone even farther and budgeted $900,000 for the development of a special college and pre-college curriculum to compensate Negroes for prior inadequacies in education and move them up to eligibility for college attendance and performance.

The on-the-job training section of the Equal Opportunity program refers mainly to a plan sponsored by the United States Department of Labor. Through contracts with individual cities, private industry may be reimbursed up to 50 per cent of a worker's salary while he is in training. The employer guarantees that he will keep the worker on after the training period is completed.

The program for local economic development is still only a project on the drawing boards. Recommendations include: the establishment of manufacturing plants in ghetto areas; guaranteed purchasing of manufactured articles by the municipality involved (e.g., the purchase of all mattresses for hospitals, shelters, and prisons by the city of Chicago from a ghetto factory); shareholding in such enterprises; the deposit of city money in ghetto-located banks; the investment of the interest on that money in ghetto businesses; the development of cooperative housing, cooperative markets, and similar undertakings that will stimulate economic growth and buying power in disadvantaged Negro areas.

The progress of the Equal Opportunity program is being watched with varying degrees of wariness or violent distaste or both by the whites and blacks who are not part of its planning or participating structure, and by some blacks who are. Every action is judged in terms of what is meant by equality; the basic conflict between the ways in which whites and blacks—as well as some blacks and other blacks—define equality becomes visible in all of its many dimensions.

White intellectual liberals have, for the most part, accepted the Equal Opportunity program. The career ladder section has a special appeal for them. It represents the traditional story of success through hard work and sacrifice that typifies for many of them the spiritual character of America. It reestablishes, too, the paternalistic relationship of the white man to the black. Watching the Negro make his way up the ladder, the white man can relax in the solacing assurance that he is still holding out a guiding hand and what is more, extending it in the direction of white tastes, white standards, white values. "God's in his heaven; All's right with the world." Things are and will be as they always have been.

But they aren't and probably never will be. As part of his definition of equality, the Negro wants to move up to full representation on supervisory, administrative, and executive work levels. His push at this upper end of the ladder has assaulted the sensibilities of many of his white liberal friends and outraged much of the rest of white society.

There are evidently a number of reasons for the white man's reaction. The most compelling would seem to be a historic emotional bias. In its informal—

but careful—ordering of status and position, America has not included a role of authority for the native Negro. The white man needs time now to assimilate a changing perspective. But time is one luxury the black man is no longer willing to allow white America. Time, in this period of decisive social ferment, is an ally the black man wants on his side.

Other reasons are more contemporary. Negro leaders openly urge a tipping of the scales in favor of the black man—both for the sake of correcting a racial imbalance and as a means of redressing previous injustices. This is hardly the way in which white people interpret equality. The more cynical among them protest candidly that their own interests in the better-paying, prestige jobs are being adversely affected. The innocents plead for justice. They still believe—intellectually, at least; they have not yet had the courage for the upheaval of more exacting soul-searching—that color was always an irrelevance, that qualifications always were and should remain the sole criteria for job selection and promotion. They sound somewhat bewildered now when they say, "I'm the best person for the job. But I won't get it. I'm the wrong color." Their anticipations are often correct. Negroes have been given preference in leadership positions in education, community organizations, poverty programs, programs dealing with Medicare, Medicaid, and many other public services. And the Negroes are not always as well qualified as the white applicants.

But there is still another reason for the exacerbation of Negro-white relationships in regard to the Equal Opportunity program. It is the "arrogance" of the black man once he is put in a position of authority. Fear, of course, may lurk behind this undue assumption of superiority that so many whites find offensive. Many blacks unfailingly see "white" as their enemy. Most blacks are still coming to grips with their identity. Placed in positions where they are sure neither of themselves nor of their relationship to whites, they fall back on an awareness of their "power" in our embattled nation. It is a grim irony that the white man is generally blind to the non-arrogant Negro, the one who makes a contribution he is well able to make and might never have had a chance to make without the Equal Opportunity program. It is an even more terrible irony that the white man fails to recognize how his greater consciousness of the arrogant Negro may well be a new mask for his prejudice, another rationalization for his reluctance to share power and position more equally with blacks.

His own fears have driven him to a stage where he sometimes seems to be witch–hunting for instances of favoritism to Negroes. The offer by the New York City Board of Education a few years ago to finance the cost of a coaching course for Negro applicants to supervisory examinations was condemned as a sellout. At the time, there were only two black principals and nine black assistant principals in the school system. Comparatively few Negroes had been applying to take the examinations. It was assumed that there were two reasons: the belief—justified or not—of eligible Negroes that the cards were being stacked against them, particularly during the oral interview part of the examination when visibility could not be avoided and "a Negro accent" sounded right as a reason for failure; the apprehension about not really being able to compete with white applicants who could usually pay the rather steep charge for a private coaching class. The invitation by the Board of Education was intended both as a reassurance to Negroes that they were wanted and a way of extending to the less affluent the benefits of concentrated preparatory cram sessions.

The more recent action by the Board to postpone an assistant principal's examination while plans were being worked out to change the requirements—from five years of regular teaching to two years of substitute and three years of regular teaching—was denounced as a lowering of standards to make possible the admission of more Negroes to the examination. This may indeed be true. It is also true that there is no very great difference between two years of preparatory work as a regular teacher and as a regular substitute and that assistant principals are badly needed. But to the white community, this is further evidence of how Negroes are moved up at the "cost of professional standards"; and the white candidates who were eligible for the originally scheduled examination have threatened the Board of Education with a lawsuit.

Other organizations seem to be more adept at working out these potentially explosive situations. A corporation may appoint a Negro to a position with an impressive title—Executive Assistant for Special Markets, for example. But the very title reveals the catch. Special markets are likely to be those where the executive assistant deals with other Negroes only. Or a city department may promote a Negro to a position of deputy commissioner. The next step is the changing of the hierarchy of responsibility. Instead of continuing to report to the deputy commissioner for direction and guidance, assistant commissioners and department heads are now instructed to go directly to the commissioner.

"With revolution," however, as Camus has put it, "awareness is born." Today's black sees this kind of equality as a further indication of the low expectations that white society has for him. He may well be furious enough to express his dissatisfaction in the vogue words of the revolutionary extremists, "Roll over, Whitey, and get out of my way!"

Negro discontent and white reluctance are not limited to the upper echelons. The white nurses, teachers, welfare investigators, librarians, and recreational workers affected by the Equal Opportunity program generally see the promotion of black people to their ranks as a kind of territorial encroachment. Their very status as whites is threatened by the black incursion. Many would gladly leave their jobs—and the uncomfortable, "arrogant" intruders—if they could. The question is, where can they go. Sammy Davis, Jr. was not talking about their plight, but he could have been, when he commented on the dilemma of white people in urban relocation. "There is just no place to hide," he said, mocking their bitterness.

Many whites on the middle income level are equally hostile to the compensatory education program. Too close usually to the economic hardships they may have experienced to feel much detachment, they deeply resent how "everything is made easy for Negroes." They are also concerned about the education of their own children. A college education loses its significance when standards are continuously scaled down to accommodate "them." Why must the Negro force his underachievement on an alien white world?

And this is precisely the question that is currently dividing the black community in America. The emphasis of the civil rights movement has been on ending segregation. It implies both the integration of the American Negro into the larger society and the extension to him of equal opportunity to make possible his full participation. The extreme black power thrust has been on a rejection of the white values that the equal opportunity program incorporates. The repudiation encompasses a number of points of view.

It may involve a contempt on the part of the black man for what he considers an academic discussion of equal rights to begin with. He can feel no great elation about his legal entrée to elegance when he doesn't have the money to pay the bill. Equal rights are his due—the answer, finally, to a moral imperative. Equal opportunity is just another one of the white man's promises. The bitter unemployed urban young Negro is not likely to see these promises in terms of a white man's education. For him, that education is one more merry-go-round leading nowhere.

For the most part, it avails little to tell him that his disillusionment is based on the past, that attitudes are different now, that education, this time, will yield him status and financial reward. He remains unconvinced. So, often, does the person doing the telling. Federal anti-poverty programs, such as the Manpower Development and Training Act and the Economic Opportunity Act (recently renamed the Adult Basic

Education Act, Title III) have, in the past, enabled only a comparative handful of Negroes to move into steady, well-paying jobs. The current equal opportunity program can reach only a limited number through its on-the-job training section and only the very young through its compensatory education provisions. The career ladder program which is likely to affect the largest number of Negroes has been budgeted by the Federal government on a year-to-year basis. Individual cities are expected to meet the cost eventually—an impossible prospect, mitigated only by the probability that Washington will have to refund the program at the end of the year.

But it is not simply rejection of the white man's faith in education that is splitting the ranks of the Negroes in regard to the Equal Opportunity program. Black racists refuse to participate in any program that is based on a concept of shared society. Their rallying cry is, "Let us get our own, own our own, run our own!" The sheer impracticality of any such large-scale plan has limited action to a minimum. There have been a few fiery suggestions for a new secession, this time through the establishment of separate Negro states in the Union, and there has been the *au naturel* movement in clothes and hair styles, a symbol of the Negro's refusal to "ape the white man," of his emphasis on doing "what's natural for black people."

No one seems to know exactly what is natural for the black man that is not so for the white. But there is no question that the black man is searching for a sense of community. The local economic development phase of the Equal Opportunity program is intended, in part, to give Negroes this community identification. Here too, however, black reaction has been mixed. Some call the plan an attempt to lead the Negro back to his compulsory ghetto. Others resent and mistrust the white man's initial share in its inception. A few doom it in advance as a palliative that will still deny the black man the opportunity he wants.

Most blacks agree that their best hope at present lies in local economic development. A black community of free enterprise can help them create jobs, build industry, develop responsibility and leadership, and work out a pattern of progress that they can then take with them to the "outside" white world. Perhaps, most important of all, it can help them to achieve the competence and self esteem they need to face this "outside."

Negro apprehension of the white world seems to be matched today by the feelings of growing uneasiness that rack the white man. It seems strange that two such negative forces may yet be the impulses that bring black man and white man together. But this is probably the basis on which communication will be established. Awareness of white anxiety has liberated the Negro from some of his own fears and strengthened his courage to demand full equality. Confrontation with Negro desperation is compelling the white man to plan for a tomorrow where the Negro will want and be able to build, not burn.

7.
YOUTH
AT BAY:
What's Happening
With Young Blacks

The serious anti-social behavior of black ghetto youth probably began in the 1940's with its highly organized inter-gang warfare. Whatever angers young people had at that time were apparently vented on each other in an emotional release that sociologists might call other-directed. In the 1950's, the hostility evidently turned inward, for youth seemed bent on destroying itself. Most of the slum gangs had been broken up but only to be replaced, it seemed, by the more unreachable problem of drug addiction. Now, nearly two decades later, the feelings have begun to turn outward. Protest—sometimes in the form of violence—is focused on the schools, the police, the landlords, the politicians—all of the powers and institutions that black ghetto youth considers responsible for its unhappiness.

Youth-serving agencies, functioning by various names throughout the country, have taken to themselves the responsibility of working with these young people. The moderate black militants who usually serve in these agencies as youth workers are themselves largely committed to moving the black revolution forward. They are pushing peaceful change, however, a task, they claim, not nearly so hopeless as some despairing souls—black and white—would maintain that it must be. But good expectations do not necessarily reduce the day-to-day tensions attending the effort.

The seething restiveness of today's black ghetto is easily triggered into open hostility. Young people are especially susceptible to the rantings which provoke them to exchange their ghetto frustrations for the temporarily healing acts of violence. They do not have the responsibilities of family obligation, job security, or social position to restrain them. Among all the ghetto blacks, they have the least to lose by their insurrection. As they see it, they also have the most to gain. Their future—as well as their present—is at stake, and at the moment it stretches before them drab, bleak, and desperate.

The revolt of the young dramatically highlights the fact that our society is in a stage of unusually swift transition. Youth is clamoring for change, a pattern of behavior its elders can perhaps philosophically shrug off as normal. The imperiousness with which boys and girls of college and even high school age assume the role of change–makers, however, is more upsetting. There is only contempt for authority and maturity in their attitudes. And the impact of their demands is disturbing the orderliness that, perhaps because it offers some sense of control over fate, helps most men feel less anxious.

Black youth workers evidence small concern in this respect. They have, of course, had precious little opportunity for control in their own lives. Their own agreement with the general tenor of the demands for change may be another reason for their lack of alarm.

Young black people are demanding change in every facet of society that affects their welfare. They are currently concentrating on three issues: their basic role as decision-makers, their part in determining educational policy and curriculum, and their definition of criteria for suitable employment.

A typical big-city youth serving agency usually operates through satellite agencies, devoted totally or in part to the problems of young people. A number of these local organizations have lately involved the young in their decision-making process with some rather unexpected results.

One group of alienated teenagers allowed to assume complete responsibility for the planning of a "hot summer" program developed a mobile library project to serve the children of elementary school age in the neighborhood. They budgeted the funds they received from the central agency, supplemented them with donations that they solicited, purchased and collected books, and rented a truck which they drove daily through the streets as a travelling library. Perhaps it is only discouraged educators who believe that ghetto youth are not really interested in books.

Another especially hostile young group, during another tense summer, worked out a cultural heritage program. They located and paid teachers, lecturers, and specialists to come and work with them in the fields of history, music, and the dance, and scheduled classes that met regularly. What is most interesting here, possibly, is that a group of young people originally almost obsessively separatist and grimly resolved to keep the "structure"—by which they meant any white person or any professional, white or black —out of their bailiwick, ended up by asking for help and being able to work with it positively.

Such isolated instances—and there are many of them—do not, of course, add up to an overwhelming tendency. But they seem significant as a possible breakthrough in the pattern of destruction and violence. They are, at any rate, hopefully accepted as such by black youth workers who continue to involve more and more young people in decision-making situations.

It is no longer unusual for black boys and girls of sixteen and over to sit with the board of directors of the community corporations, the governing boards of the local anti-poverty programs. Young people may serve on committees assigned to such areas as health, narcotics, housing, model cities, education, Head Start, safety, sanitation, employment, family planning, and Golden Age needs. On one of these committees, the young people suggested that they be given the charge of working with rebellious children in a remedial reading program—an offer which may not meet with the full professional approval of reading experts, but which is certainly heartening as an example of successful motivation of potential young troublemakers. On another committee, it was the young people who urged the development of a preventive narcotics program for a community where the adult members of the committee did not even know the extent of the problem. Negro youth, it seems, can bring attention to dormant issues by its involvement and possibly help society to confront difficulties before the abandonment to despair takes over.

The interest of young people in educational involvement has been dramatized by the unprecedented and, in some cases, shockingly destructive, sit-ins which made the colleges and universities the target of their widespread attacks. In many of these demonstrations, both Negro and white students protested for the admission of more black students to universities, for a greater student voice in curriculum making and in determining the policies of student discipline, and for an opportunity to evaluate their teaching staff. Black college students have demanded schools of black studies, black student social organizations, black dormitories and school cafeteria tables to be designated for the use of blacks only. Their insistence on this separateness, they maintain, is motivated by their need to relax in a setting where they are not regarded as curiosities or continuously probed about the race problem by over-eager white liberals who still do not know how to relate to fellow black students as equals. The experience at Williams College in Williams, Massachusetts, where many of these demands were met by the administration, may well be significant as a trend, however. All of the forty black students registered in the college actively participated in the protest; only nine of them have availed themselves of their new separatist privileges.

Black college students have expressed, too, their right to take part in the educational planning for young Negro children. They have recommended that they act as the board of directors for at least one experimental junior high school in a black urban community. They have incorporated their ideas into a proposal which they have forwarded for Federal funding to the Title I office of the Department of Health, Education, and Welfare in Washington.

The idea may not be as far out as at first glance it seems. Negro college students can be expected to identify with blacks who are not much younger than they are, to understand their learning deterrents and to respond to their learning potential. Their own confrontation with the educational process qualifies them more than some Negro parents who are school board members to set up standards and give advice about the educational importance of one course or another. Their very presence as young blacks who are succeeding can be a source of educational excitement. When they are male blacks, they may also supply the strong father figure that is missing from the lives of many Negro children.

What may seem even more radical is the growing demand by black junior and senior high school students to be involved in the planning of their own educational program. This has become standard practice in a number of urban schools, where students meet with administrators periodically to tell what they think. At most such meetings, they have expressed a need for more contemporary and more relevant training. For example, in the field of mathematics, they want to know about interest computation in terms of paying for a car. In social studies, they want to learn how to "beat the structure." Their specific questions are: "What do we do to get the landlord to paint?"

"Where do we go to ask for better garbage collection?" "How do we go about getting a play street?" Actually, they are asking for information about the orderly processes of democratic change. They are challenging the schools to provide them with the tools of democratic community effort and with the skills—as in the mathematics example—for managing their lives as they know them.

They have revealed, too, in these interchanges between students and educators, what may perhaps be considered—at this point in American history, at any rate—a learning style that is seemingly characteristic of ghetto blacks. It appears to tend more to action than to abstraction. It leans on community traditions of informal know-how, peer learning, hip language, and the probability of foreseeable vocational success. Except for the last, these are concepts which can easily be translated into educational approaches that may prove more attuned to the personalities and strengths of the learners. The success factor must depend, in part, on the reality of job prospects.

"Long bread," the vernacular for good money, seems to be the main criterion for employment among the black ghetto youth. They are quick to define their terms when a job or training for a job is offered to them. They want long bread during and after the training period. Cynicism about the white man's intentions discourages many of them from accepting long-term training. They put much greater reliance on the money in their pockets than on the white man's promises. They have learned that lesson from history, they say.

Some, not quite so bitter, are more patient with

themselves and with society. They are eager to develop the skills which will enable them to compete as equals with their white peer groups. Their ambitions are varied: to teach, to preach, to become businessmen, to develop political leadership, to work in the skilled trades, to function on managerial or executive levels. Quite a few of these young Negroes want essentially to train themselves so that they can come back and help the black ghetto community. They, too, are realists. They believe that neither force nor reform will quickly eliminate the ills of the urban ghetto.

An increasing number of young black people are accepting the educational opportunities that are opening up to prepare them for their chosen vocations. Many of the programs are competitive from the very beginning, demanding of the black student the same standards of excellence as from the white. Prestige prep schools such as Andover, Hotchkiss, Milton, and Westminster are cooperating with A Better Chance, more generally known as the ABC program. They are admitting Negroes for college preparation and offering scholarships on an as–needed basis. High–ranking colleges are admitting blacks to work-study programs. The government pays 90 per cent of the needed costs and the university or employer the rest. The much publicized Upward Bound program, which admits underachievers to city universities with free tuition and a stipend for living expenses, is one of the very many compensatory plans that are being organized for the disadvantaged young Negro.

All of this training effort seems to be concentrated on helping the young black get into the mainstream of American society, a desirable goal from the white liberal's point of view and from that of the large majority of Negroes. In the long run, this is what the black revolution is all about. The American Negro wants the same privileges and good fortune that most white citizens enjoy. He maintains that the effects of white supremacy have robbed him of the prerogative of equal opportunity. He now demands for himself the right to exert power over his own destiny. For the most part, he hopes to achieve both power and the good growing out of it through viable channels for change, that is, through responsive political representation, significant economic development in black communities, and meaningful individual upward mobility. It is usually only blacks with completely hopeless feelings about the white man's willingness or emotional ability to accept such mobility who call so insistently for separatism.

Young Negro inductees into the white intellectual establishment, where prejudice tends to be lower, more often than not emerge with greater confidence in themselves and in a future which includes working within the white structure. When imbued with a sense of commitment to the black revolution—and most of them are—they are likely to use their strengths to work harder for change, preferably without violence. They know very well that violence can be used to destroy white indifference and even to evoke long overdue concessions. But they understand that it can also produce fear and counterviolence and demolish good as well as evil. They are optimistic enough to see some good in the American way of life.

This faith, of course, is in direct contrast to the philosophy of the hippies who want to withdraw as far as possible from the "establishment." Young hippie revolutionaries protest against the establishment's "trick bag" of competitive ambitions and "institutional" jobs and conformity to such lures as the house in the suburbs, the five o'clock cocktail, and what used to be called the gray flannel suit. They find it more personally satisfying to work, for example, as janitors—when they do work—because this, at least, is honest labor, and to live communally, enjoying the simple pleasures that money cannot buy.

The young black revolutionary has had no taste of conformity—unless one counts the dreary sameness of grinding poverty and the hopeless monotony of white rejection, overt or unconscious. At this moment, he would probably like nothing better than to have an opportunity to live with the "trick bag" and the chances are that he would enjoy it just fine. But then the black revolutionary does not have the same background as the hippie. It is common knowledge that most hippie rebels come from solid, even affluent middle and upper-class homes. Very few Negroes are hippies. On occasion, young blacks have even expressed their resentment against hippie play-acting with poverty by mugging and rolling the young white rebels who can always go home to Darien.

In our troubled century, there can doubtless be many different kinds of revolution for social change occurring on several levels of society. Most of them will probably have young people as their standard bearers. But it is the revolution that the young ghetto black may ignite that is of the gravest concern to white and black America right now. The feeling still remains among most young ghetto blacks, as it does with the members of the President's "Riot Commission," that despite all the turmoil and efforts among concerned citizens and officials, nothing has really changed for them.

It does little good to review with them the strides that have been and are being made to include them in decent jobs and in training for skilled and professional employment, to explain that the National Alliance of Business Men has been organized specifically to help ghetto youth get jobs and job training in private enterprise, and that the Urban Coalition was created for ghetto needs. They know that none of this has as yet touched them personally. Despite the advantages available to some Negro ghetto youth, the fact is that the large majority remain uninvolved in the educational and employment programs that have been developed.

White recalcitrance—the kind that makes Congress slow to move on measures important to the Negro and many communities even slower in implementing legislation intended to benefit him—and the Negro's impatience for change may combine to constitute the underlying causes of black ghetto restiveness. But almost any incident can precipitate the battle. Black ghetto youth seems, at times, just to be waiting for the signal to begin the national agony of the looting and the burning.

No one actually does give the signal. The riots of the young ghetto blacks do not appear to be planned outbursts, aimed at a specific objective and responding to the direction of a leader. On the contrary, they seem to erupt as sudden expressions of release from that which is no longer tolerable. The potential proportions of the explosion are frightening even to some of the extremist revolutionaries. They, too, went out into the streets to plead for order after Dr. King's assassination. In New York, CORE and other militants worked with more moderate Negro representatives to dispel rumors, quiet flare-ups, and minimize mob action. In Newark, LeRoi Jones switched from advocating violence to calling on the black community to take over the city by ballots. Five hundred young blacks patrolled the areas of worst disorder to try to persuade other Negro young people to "cool it."

Control over disorders would conceivably be simpler if there were leaders with whom to bargain, deal, or negotiate. They could, at least, give a countersignal for the cessation of hostilities while talks were taking place. As it is, the negotiations have to be conducted practically on a one-to-one basis, the peacemakers going from one angry youth to another or from one irate group of young people to the next in an effort to get them to listen to reason.

The tendency these days seems to be for black ghetto youth to listen most to those who agitate the loudest. Hope doesn't cool anyone any more. Young Negroes want change here and now. For the large majority, a good job right away or an immediate apprenticeship to a job with undeniably good prospects is the only meaningful beginning. It is their symbol of society's awakened responsibility. It is the important concrete evidence of the affirmation of their black power.

8.
EXPLOSION
IN THE
SCHOOLS

The social unrest which apparently characterizes America's current mood is probably epitomized in the discord dominating most of the country's big city school systems. The 1954 Supreme Court decision denying the doctrine of separate but equal schools may have provided the backdrop for this particular drama. It was a routine news item released to the nation's press, however, that put the actors in motion. In 1963, the New York City Board of Education made public its statistics about pupil achievement as measured by standardized tests. Grade by grade, school by school, district by district, ghetto children—meaning here largely Negro children—were behind in reading and mathematics. Reading skills began to fall behind by the time a child was in about the third grade. And they continued to fall. By the fourth grade, a ghetto child was usually a year behind his non-ghetto peers in reading. By the sixth grade, he was two years behind; by the ninth grade, the lag was about three years. A directive from the Superintendent of Schools requiring a ninth grade reading level for a high school diploma—by which time twelve school grades have been completed—met with local consternation. Ghetto high school principals pleaded for time to try to get their graduating classes up to this ninth year minimum.

Statistics gathered for the larger area of the Metropolitan Northeast are only a little more hopeful. In the critical skills of reading and verbal ability, Negro students fall farther behind whites with each year of school completed. They begin the first grade with somewhat lower scores than whites on standard achievement tests, are about 1.6 grades behind by the sixth grade, and have fallen 3.3 grades behind the white pupils by the twelfth grade.

National figures reflect the same discouraging lack of basic skills among Negro youth. During the period June 1964—December 1965, 67 per cent of the Negro candidates failed the Selective Service qualifying test. The failure rate for whites was 19 per cent.

Reaction from the Negro community to the New York City statistics was instantaneous. This large metropolitan school system was, in the opinion of most Negro educators, typical of urban education everywhere. A diagnosis of its critical failings could undoubtedly serve with some modifications for urban educational systems throughout the country. A plan to narrow the gap between the educational achievements of Negro children as compared with white children might offer a suitable model for Newark, Chicago, Detroit, or Los Angeles.

The debate over the best ways to bridge this gap has been on-going and tumultuous ever since. To date, the Negro protagonists have suggested, in turn, three solutions. The first was the battle to overcome de facto segregation in education.

In 1963, most New York City schools could be identified as black or white. The educational system was built on an affection for the "warm, friendly" neighborhood school. Most Negroes, living in a Negro neighborhood, sent their children to a Negro neighborhood school.

But Negro neighborhood schools, according to the black community, failed to meet the criteria which are generally regarded as indicators of good educational quality. Negro schools had fewer regular teachers than the white schools, a larger number of inexperienced teachers, a greater teacher turnover, a higher teacher absentee rate, shabbier—sometimes decrepit—equipment, and not enough suitable books, libraries, and laboratories. In all these tangible ways, the Negro community maintained, their ghetto schools were separate and UNequal; an accusation, among others, that the establishment evidently considered serious enough to warrant official investigation. Section 402 of the 1964 Civil Rights Act called for a survey and a report to the President and to the Congress "concerning the lack of availability of equal educational opportunities for individuals by reason of race, color, religion, or national origin in the public educatonal institutions at all levels in the United States." A committee, headed by James S. Coleman of Johns Hopkins University, was assigned to make the study.

The push of the black ghetto community in those

comparatively halcyon days was for the integration of their children in the better white schools. The New York City Board of Education responded with its rezoning and busing programs.

Rezoning meant redefining the areas of responsibility of the local schools. A particular school district could be rezoned, for example, to run from east to west instead of from north to south, to include the middle and upper-class children—who might be living at the eastern or western extremes—in the same school with the poorer children who were at the district's center. The sanctity of the neighborhood school was being carefully maintained. It was only the concept of neighborhood that was changing. Parents who objected to the new boundary lines had two relatively simple alternatives: they could move someplace where rezoning had not yet caught on as an approach to school integration; or they could transfer their children to private or parochial schools. They did both in unanticipated numbers. The mass migration out of the city by middle-class families, the unprecedented burgeoning of private schools, and the bursting registrations in parochial schools that may have started in the 1950's certainly received a new impetus with school rezoning in the early 1960's.

In the black ghetto, rezoning could not offer even a partial solution toward integration. Where blacks and only blacks lived, no maneuvering of district lines could reach out to encompass white children. Busing Negro children out of the ghetto and into the nearest white school seemed the only practical step to take.

By and large, the white community was less than receptive to in-busing. Loudly complaining pickets paraded up and down the entrance to the Board of Education Brooklyn headquarters. White parents carried signs expressing their loyalty to the unsullied neighborhood school and, incidentally, their worry about the fatiguing effects of travel on young ghetto children. The Negro community did not buy the unsolicited concern. It did not fail to observe, either, the more furtive actions by white parents too shy—and in many cases too ashamed—to walk this picket line. A number were following their ex-neighbors to housing in or near the suburbs or making discreet inquiries about the cost of private schools.

Principals of white schools were also protesting that their buildings were too crowded to accommodate in-busing. Negro parents who had some awareness of the manipulative potential in statistics called this move the numbers game. Suggestions that white children might be transferred out of such schools to achieve maximum desegration and to relieve overcrowding could not have been more at variance with prevailing white sentiment. White mothers were ready to man machine guns over that issue. And white principals were not above asking their pupils such loaded questions as, "Who wants to leave this lovely school that we have here? If you do, raise your hands." Naturally, virtually no one ever did.

Some principals solved the problem of integration to the satisfaction of even the most vociferous white parents. In the elementary and junior high schools, they simply maintained an in-bused group of Negro children—usually from one school grade—as a separate class. In the high schools, all they had to do was to follow the track system. The aptitude tests, geared to a middle-class culture, automatically placed most Negro students in the commercial or general track where they had little contact with the "better" students in the school population.

And so they remained, separate and definitely UN-equal—for a high school commercial or general education was not intended to be as full or as enriching as that provided in the upper track, and on the elementary and junior high school levels a class of in-bused ghetto children was not exactly the middle-class teacher's cup of tea. Many teachers assigned to these classes found them "unteachable" and sooner or later gave up. Either they resigned, as most had in the ghetto schools (between 1952 and 1962, almost half the licensed teachers of New York City left the system), or they stayed on and stopped trying.

The intangibles of teacher attitudes can be as humiliating as outright segregation. And most of the in-bused Negro children were defensive to begin with. Even when placed in non-segregated classes, they tended to cling to one another. At recess, at lunch tables, in the groups they formed outside of the schools, blacks generally stayed with blacks. Both their common background and their mutual resentfulness drew them together. They felt themselves different from the white children. They were not nearly so verbal or so replete with experiences—of the kind that can be related in a white school—to be verbal about. Curriculum and materials appeared to have little connection with their lives. Those black children who did not withdraw into apathy fought to assert themselves in their own way. Behavioral deviations created serious disciplinary problems. These disrupted the learning climate and frequently demoralized even the best-intentioned of classroom teachers. The problem was often compounded by the fact that some of the in-bused children had come with emotional difficulties and that there were no adequate resources for their care.

Dr. Coleman stated in the report which he completed in 1965 that Negro students perform better in comfortably integrated schools. He also said that if a white pupil from a home strongly and effectively supportive of education is put in a school where most pupils do not come from such homes, his achievement will be little different from what it would be if he were in a school composed of others like himself. But Negro students, from all appearances, were hardly comfortable in the majority of the white schools to which they had been bused. And most white parents were too fearful and impatient to put much faith in the assurances of Dr. Coleman or of other educators who had more informally come to the same conclusions. Integration, on the whole, was failing.

The Negro community turned its attention to a second solution, that of improving the standards and practices of separate ghetto schools. The New York City Board of Education was only too ready to cooperate. Quality education became, almost overnight, its slogan. For one thing, it was probably glad to get off the in-busing hook. For another, continued population shifts were making this kind of integration increasingly impractical. Relatively affluent whites were steadily leaving the city to be replaced by more and more Negroes with larger families of school-age children. It was a national pattern. Between 1961 and 1965, Detroit's Negro public school enrollment increased by 31,108 while white enrollment increased by 23,748. In Cincinnati between 1960 and 1965, the Negro population grew 16 per cent and the Negro public school enrollment increased 26 per cent. Negroes now have a majority or near majority of public school students in seven of the ten largest American cities, as well as in other cities. Figures for 1965-1966 show a 90.9 percentage of Negro students in public elementary school enrollment in Washington, D.C., a 69.1 percentage in Newark, and a 63.3 percentage in St. Louis.

The New York City Board of Education did not wholly abandon its integration efforts. Official policy still condoned open enrollment—the opportunity for Negro parents to register their children in a school other than a neighborhood school if they liked, and if the school they preferred was not already overcrowded. Most Negro parents found this practice too taxing emotionally or too burdensome physically to take much advantage of it. The Board is also going ahead with its development of the comprehensive high school, intended to end the isolation of largely black vocational high schools. It has not given up its plans for the pairing of white and non-white schools, each to accommodate black and white children of different age groups; or of its hopes for school parks—educational complexes designed to encompass schools on varying levels with children from many neighborhoods —perhaps a more natural step in the integration process. But quality education became in 1964 its central thrust.

⤷ The Higher Horizons program, initiated at Junior High School 43, Manhattan in 1956, to find and encourage students with college potential in a disadvantaged community, served to some degree as a precedent for the quality education idea. The Board could not hope to duplicate the extent of the services that had been put at the disposal of Junior High School 43 on the scale it now anticipated. But it could make an attempt.

Of the 755 elementary and junior high schools then in the New York City school system, 176 were designated in 1957 (there were 287 of them at the beginning of 1969) as special service schools, on the basis of pupils' reading and language limitations. All were schools in poverty areas where a great number of the the parents received welfare assistance, virtually every child was eligible for free lunches, and school truancy, as well as high student turnover, came almost to represent a norm. Special service schools were and continue to be staffed with extra personnel to reduce class size and with additional teaching, guidance, supervisory, and administrative services. Tutorial programs have been instituted. Larger allotments have been provided for texts and supplies. And a special emphasis has been given to field trips, both for enriching the child's experiential background, and through visits to the Countee Cullen Library, for example, for improving his self–image.

The More Effective Schools program started in 1964, is a still more concentrated effort in the direction of compensatory education. Emphasis in each of the twenty-one MES schools is placed on intensive teacher preparation, individualized instruction, and specialized personnel to improve services. Classes are small. The current proportion is one staff member—including teachers, teacher aides, teacher specialists in reading and other curriculum areas, psychologists, psychiatrists, and social workers—to ten children.

No one has doubted the sound intentions of the MES program. Its achievements are not quite so certain. One recent study showed no marked improvement in the reading or mathematics scores of the children. Another—this one, a rigidly controlled longitudinal approach where the same group was tested periodically over a period of time—indicated that the MES groups made greater gains than the control groups. Both studies may be more significant in the perspective of previous research which showed that MES children, before coming into the program, had on the average been improving only six months during any school year; they fell more and more behind the national norms during every succeeding school year. In the opinion of many teachers, this consideration lends more promise to the MES program. Evidently their faith has been justified, for the recently published 1968 reading scores show more than half of the MES pupils at or above grade levels.

But the Negro community has done an about–face on compensatory education. It isn't that Negro parents and educators want to increase class size or to reduce the number or extent of auxiliary services. It's just that they no longer believe in the underlying philosophy of compensatory education. They say that teachers have negative attitudes toward their children and that, as Dr. Kenneth Clark puts it, "Children who are treated as if they are uneducable invariably become uneducable." They quote the experience of the white teacher who was given the misinformation that one of her Mexican-American classes was much brighter than the other; the class assumed to be brighter did much better than the supposedly duller group, and—as an additional commentary, this one on the expectations of identification—the performance of the light–complexion children surpassed that of the dark–skinned pupils in the same "bright" class. Negroes protest, too, that the current educational practices of correcting "Negro" speech, which is really regional dialect shared by Negroes and whites, and of criticizing by the implications of comparison the appearance or habits or background of black children, deprives them of any motivating sense of self–worth. In essence, their objections are to a system that makes the child fit into the white middle-class school. And in New York City, the Negro community has decided to take matters into its own hands and to make the school fit the life experiences, interests, and needs of the black child.

Community control of education through decentralization is the third solution black people are offering to improve the school achievement of their children. In terms of the hostilities and struggles it has evoked, this solution may well be the most controversial of them all.

The decentralization of a large metropolitan school system would under ordinary circumstances attract minor attention and certainly create little dissent. The New York City system had grown to a size that even

its Superintendent called "monstrous and overbear-
ing." Critics more inclined to specify pointed to the
breakdown in communication between the policy
makers and the lower echelons, the inadequate awareness at central headquarters of local school needs, the
evident lack of responsiveness to community conditions, and all the other big and small failings that
follow in the wake of an overextended administration.
In May 1967, the Board of Education adopted a
decentralization plan; it went on to increase local
powers in October 1967. The thirty existing district
advisory school boards could now recommend, subject to the Superintendent's approval, their own district superintendents. And in consultation with this
superintendent, a district could choose its own principals and allocate its own funds. As a hopefully
peaceful resolution of the issue of educational control
by local black communities, the Board's action came
rather late.

Negro bitterness about the education that black
children were receiving had been steadily mounting.
Some hope still existed in 1965 and 1966 when Harlem's new Intermediate School 201 was going up on
East 128 Street. The Board had promised that it
would be an integrated school—which meant to
Harlem that it would be a better staffed and more
fully equipped school. According to Negro community leaders, the Board had pledged that white
children would be bused in from Queens across the
nearby Triborough Bridge. When the reactive up-
roar in Queens clearly placed such a possibility in the
realm of fantasy, the Board sent Puerto Rican children
—from their own ghetto—instead. This was next to

the last straw. The last one seems to have been some statement by the Board to the effect that this admixture of Negro and Puerto Rican children represented the integration that had been intended all along. It was at this point in September 1966, on the day when I.S. 201 was scheduled to open, that the black community rebelled. "If this is going to be a black school," the Negro parents said, "we, the blacks, are going to run it."

The Negro community has been rebelling ever since. Black extremists have taken up the battle cry, urging parents to insist on "black power," describing district superintendents as "colonizers," and organizing, first their own "People's Board of Education" to sit for twenty-four hours, symbolically, in the Board of Education board room, and then their "little people's boards" to take the place of the established district boards. Mayor John Lindsay joined the fray when Albany advised him that more state aid for education depended on the plan he would submit for needed school decentralization. McGeorge Bundy, president of the Ford Foundation, accepted the role of heading a committee to prepare such a plan. Even before he went to work on this committee, he persuaded the Ford Foundation—this was in June 1967—to finance four decentralization demonstration districts in New York City. One of these has since involved the United Federation of Teachers in the battle—on the opposing side—chiefly over the issue of teacher tenure.

Both I.S. 201 and the eight elementary schools that feed into it in Harlem and the two intermediate schools with their six feeder schools in Ocean Hill-Brownsville were designated as Board of Education demonstration units. A third unit, centered around the Joan of Arc Junior High School on Manhattan's West 93rd Street, was planned. The fourth, known as the Two Bridges unit, on the lower East Side, interrupted operations temporarily when its unit administrator, frustrated by his limited authority, resigned and the neighborhood parents' associations voted to return the schools to the jurisdiction of the district superintendent. It subsequently resumed functioning again as an experimental unit.

One of the determining factors in the success or failure of the experimental units is undoubtedly the power of their governing boards. As organized by the Ford Foundation, each unit had a governing board composed of parents, teachers, and community representatives, which replaced the district board of education. The governing board was to choose its own unit administrator to replace the district superintendent, to set educational goals and standards for its own schools, and to recruit and select staff. In theory, these seem the reasonable responsibilities of a decentralized school district. In practice, each responsibility implies powers that have been heatedly contested against a background of differing values, ambitions, and interests, vested or otherwise.

The recruitment and selection of staff, reflecting the conflict of interest between the governing boards on the one side and, in this case, the Board of Education and the United Federation of Teachers on the other, and affecting, as it must, the goals and standards of schools, has probably constituted the most contested responsibility. The conflict is perhaps sharpened by the fact that a majority of the governing boards at

both I.S. 201 and Ocean Hill-Brownsville were black
and by the possibility that they were not uninfluenced
by the extremist blacks who champion their cause.
It hardly seems an accident that Floyd McKissick,
while he was still director of CORE, spoke at the I.S.
201 graduation exercises; or that Herman Ferguson,
by now convicted of conspiring to murder moderate
Negro leaders, acted, in turn, as community advisory
member to the governing board at I.S. 201 designated
by the Governing Board and as principal of I.S. 55 in
Ocean Hill-Brownsville. Blacks have replied that they
would naturally support a Floyd McKissick or a Herman Ferguson, both of whom had been attacked by
the white community for their commitment to the
black revolution. It was a question of taking sides.

Critics of the decentralized units, agreeing that
such choices are indeed natural, have accused the
governing boards of wanting to hire as many Negroes
as they could regardless of qualifications, and of trying to reshape their school curricula in the direction
of black racism, rather than in the pursuit of quality
education. The standard answer of the governing
board was that the white establishment never did
supply their children with education which was
quality for them and that the development of black
pride may need to precede other learning.

Professionals jealously guard the criteria which have
given them their standing and fight against every
effort by the experimental units to change established
job qualifications. One of the disputes in this area
concerned the right of unit administrators to recommend for the position of school principal persons who
had not taken or passed the competitive examinations

that are mandated by state law. The Board of Education went along with this innovation at Ocean Hill-Brownsville, approving all except one recommendation. The Council of Supervisory Associations, protecting its own interests, instituted legal action. A trial and appeals court declared the appointment of principals without the mandatory examination illegal, but this decision was reversed by the New York State Supreme Court. The ruling applied only to demonstration districts.

The most explosive dispute arose over the decision by the Ocean Hill-Brownsville unit in May 1968 to transfer thirteen teachers, five assistant principals, and one principal from its district. This produced immediate cross fire from the Board of Education, which demanded due process for its staff members, from the United Federation of Teachers, which asserted that its city-wide union contract controls all assignment of instructional personnel in the units, and from the Council of Supervisory Associations, which for the first time in its history allied itself with the teachers' organization. The timing of the decision, just before the Albany legislature was to vote on the various decentralization plans, including the Bundy report, and the very provocativeness of the challenge suggest that the dismissals were a deliberate test of unit authority.

It seems a pity, "Liberal" whites say that the unit found it necessary to raise an issue which so frightened and alienated the professional staff. Teachers, threatened by what they believed to be loss of tenure and pension rights in a system where they could be arbitrarily dismissed from one district and left without salary or pension continuity while they sought work in another—these teachers moved immediately to defend themselves. A United Federation of Teachers lobby helped to defeat the decentralized legislation ('the Regents' plan) that the experimental units most wanted. Instead, they got a law which put off for another year any complete plan for school decentralization and provided an interim decentralization bill which gave local school boards, including the demonstration projects, the right to exercise any powers granted to them by law and delegated to them by the Board of Education.

The three autumn strikes by the United Federation of Teachers, later joined by the Council of Supervisory Associations, were organized labor's response to the continued refusal of the Ocean Hill-Brownsville governing board and unit administrator to take back the nineteen educators it had "ousted" in May, to the "harassment" of these educators by the community and by "outside agitators," and to the maneuvers of the Ocean Hill-Brownsville governing board and unit administrator for keeping the seventy-nine unwanted teachers—who had walked out in May in support of the nineteen—from resuming their classroom assignments in Ocean Hill-Brownsville's eight schools. Actually, three hundred and fifty teachers had walked out but most preferred not to return to Ocean Hill-Brownsville. As the strikes progressed and the Council of Supervisory Associations became more active, the Ocean Hill-Brownsville retention of unlicensed school principals became another area of vociferous dispute —though perhaps not an official strike issue.

The underlying cause of the three strikes, as the labor organizations saw it, was the protection of their members. The nineteen educators had received notice of their immediate "transfer" by telegram, with no specification of reasons, no prior opportunity for the usual discussion, and no provision for legal due process. From the local governing board's point of view, the central issue was the right to complete community control, a concept which included the privilege of excluding "unsympathetic" teachers and evoked deep resentment about striking teachers who "had walked out on our children" without previous notice. While pickets marched and police patrolled and a Board of Education was temporarily enlarged—by the mayor to thirteen members as per the interim decentralization plan—and now contained a highly vocal group openly supporting community control, the divisiveness grew stronger and ever more hostile. Strikers made accusations of mob rule and of threatened or actual violence. Rhody McCoy and his allies talked of "cultural genocide" directed by white teachers against Negro pupils and of a "conspiracy" to stunt and destroy the minds of black children. Mr. McCoy issued a statement declaring, "It is no longer reasonable to expect that black people will . . . submit to a genocidal system." Mr. Carson, formerly of Brooklyn CORE and visibly active as one of the "outside agitators," said during an interview that "certain teachers have conspired to miseducate the black and Puerto Rican children." Mr. Ferguson, also making a charge of educational genocide, this time about the teachers in a Harlem school, made no mention of the fact that students in that school, before it became part of a decentralized unit, had reading scores substantially above the grade level; nor did he indicate any awareness of the statistics showing that the Brooklyn I.S. 271 students had improved their reading scores by three years and seven months in the period of two years and ten months when I.S. 271 was under the supervision of a white principal.

The strike settlement in November 1968 guaranteed the safe return of the disputed educators to their regular assignments in the district and placed the Ocean Hill-Brownsville unit under a state trusteeship to insure the orderly resumption of keeping school. This in no way, however, ended the conflict about black community control. And the New York State legislature which passed a compromise school decentralization bill on April 30, 1969 did little in this direction, either. The new law provides for: employment and placement of educational personnel by the central Board of Education; a limited role in curriculum development by local boards; absorption of the demonstration districts into the new structure of thirty-three local school districts; a new interim central Board of Education, consisting of one member appointed by each of the five borough presidents, to serve for a period of one year; and a new seven-member board, five to be elected—again one from each borough— and two to be appointed by the mayor for a four-year term. A disapproving black community, anticipating no black representation through elections in boroughs where voters are predominantly white—though this may be mitigated by the provision for voting on the basis of proportional representation—is now concentrating on three courses of action: intensive training of black local school board members in the maximum use of their legal powers; the achievement of a large black vote as a show of strength in central Board of Education elections; and the rallying of black forces for gathering state political support in favor of a stronger community-controlled school system.

That a more completely decentralized school system, as a less cumbersome means of responding to local needs, must eventually become a reality in most large urban areas seems inevitable. The fate of total black control—and the issue has already extended to Chicago, Detroit, and Philadelphia and is likely to keep arising elsewhere—is not so certain. Misinformed state legislatures may be negatively influenced—as they may well have been in New York—by reported extremist positions such as that of Herman Ferguson, who in his "black survival curriculum" for a people's school, advocated the pledge of allegiance to his red, black, and green flag, the teaching of mathematics through weaponry techniques, and a required course of military training for blacks. Or they may use as a criterion the experience of the three New York City demonstration districts where racism and separatism—both black and Puerto Rican—seemed to be riding high. Self-assertion was obviously the need of the hour. Blacks concentrated on Africa; Puerto Ricans on Spanish. A story in *The New York Times* told about the demonstration unit principal who reprimanded a Puerto Rican child for answering him in English, rather than in Spanish—this, in a New York City school where the learning of English as a second language is a major problem in the education of Spanish-speaking children. Good teachers and principals were not inclined to remain in schools where their sincere ethnic commitment was often challenged in terms of the time they spent on African or Puerto Rican culture, important as these curriculum areas might admittedly be. And student turnover, in a situation characterized more by learning –time lost through boycotts, sit-ins, walkouts, and counter–walkouts than by opportunities to develop possibly significant educational innovations, was unusually high. Actually, educational progress could not be measured in this transitional and highly exploratory period.

And state legislatures may consider the Coleman report, which states categorically that achievement by minority students is consistently highest in the Metropolitan North, and it is commonly known that it is in the Metropolitan North that white middle-class teachers abound; the lack of achievement in the South must, however, take into account such factors as the poor quality of most Negro schools, including the colleges where the majority of black teachers have been receiving their training. Or these legislators may cite further educational research which points up the fact that minority children perform better in an integrated classroom than in a majority Negro school because of the stimulation of better peer achievement and higher teacher expectations.

But before making their decisions, these arbiters about city educational systems need to give serious thought to the inequities that have been imposed by a white society on its black minority and to understand the relationship of the inequities to the current black educational demands. The schools, to quote Coleman again, can "bring little influence to bear on a child's achievement that is independent of his family background and social context." Still, the schools, as one fighting front in a black revolution which battles simultaneously against family, social, and economic deprivations can help a black child to develop pride in himself and his history and extend to him the realistic hope of a future where schooling will make self-fulfillment possible. Most proponents of black community control see this third solution for the education of black ghetto children as the only way of eventually integrating them on terms of adult equality in the American scene. By their own statement of goals, these blacks have defined themselves as non-separatist. Their struggle for control over black schools seems to be rather a cynical acceptance of the present fact of black–white separation and a plan for providing black children with the kind of education that ultimately reduces this separation to a minimum. One of the crucial issues during the growing pains period, however, remains the question as to whether the extremist or his more moderate soul brother will call the educational shots should community control of education become a fact in the increasingly black-populated urban areas of America.

9.
NOT
NEXT DOOR:
Housing

In terms of the emotions it arouses, integrated housing seems to rank only a little below miscegenation on the terror list of most white Americans. The heads of white households have been known to give up even their hoarded rent-controlled apartments at the sight —or the rumor—of more than one Negro family moving into the neighborhood. Some of these whites are avowed liberals, sympathetic to the Negro cause, generous with their financial contributions, ready, as a matter of fact, to do anything for the black man— anything, except to live near him.

The black man, for his part, has no special desire to live near whites. His push for integrated housing is motivated by two factors entirely unrelated to his feeling for or about white people: a need to move out of the sub-standard housing in which one half of America's non–white population lives and into a

neighborhood where such services as schools, hospitals, sanitation, and police protection are likely to
be better; and a very natural desire for the freedom to
choose his address in accordance with the dictates of
his taste and his pocketbook. In both instances, integrated housing, that is in this context, housing outside the Negro ghetto, has for a long time been the
black man's only alternative. Idealists committed to
anti-discriminatory practices have hoped to use integrated housing as a means of breaking down both
the national patterns of segregation and the historic
anti-Negro feelings that usually underlie them.

Efforts by city agencies to improve the housing
available to urban Negroes and to develop more integrated communities concentrated initially on the
poor. The first step was the erection of what blacks
sometimes refer to as concrete jungles. These are the
enormous institution-like buildings that stretch for
block after block in a ghetto or on its fringes and are
so easily recognized as low-income projects. One out
of every five or six Negroes in New York City lives in
a project. The proportion is probably about the same
in all central cities. Many Negroes prefer to live outside of the project rather than to submit to the invasion of privacy that the stringent rules and regulations so often entail. Many do not get in because
there are just not enough projects available or because
they are earning a few dollars more than the maximum
qualifying them for admission. And some are clearly
not project desirables. These are the criminals, perverts, prostitutes, and dope peddlers or users, who
rarely apply because of the fear of identification,
and the families that are simply too large for even

the biggest project apartments. All of these persons remain in the slum that often rings the project or extends from it back into the ghetto. The personal deterioration in the slum outside of the project presents problems for which there are no ready answers; better housing is obviously not even the beginning of one. Slum proximity to the project encourages relationships which have their effects in violence and drug addiction on project residents, as well.

But the project also provides its own climate for unsocial behavior. Intended to replace the ghetto, it has become instead another version of the same slum enclosure. Its sidewalks may be a little cleaner—a result of the unremitting efforts of its clean-up crews —and its windows much bigger, but the separation from the larger society remains intact. Low-income projects house, of course, only the poor. In inner cities, the percentage of Negro and Puerto Rican tenants may be as high as 98 per cent. The group isolation is intensified by a personal one apparently growing out of a reluctance to indulge in the neighborliness that often makes ghetto life bearable. But then, non-project ghetto residents have little to hide from each other. In a project, it is the rare tenant who has not at one time or another violated at least one of the rules laid down by a housing authority. Community bonds have no opportunity to develop when the prevailing sentiment seems to be "The less your neighbors know about you, the better."

There has been one notable exception to this social isolation. In the heyday of neighborhood gangs, teen–age project boys organized some of the best. They did it with no great effort. The potential recruits were all there on the premises. And no other young people were around to challenge their decision, to offer a differing set of values, or to provide an image of another way to live. Low-income projects—as well, of course, as some parts of middle-class surburbia—are unique in their concentration on such restrictive homogeneity.

To some degree, city housing authorities have been forced into economic and color patterning. Income specifications for eligibility have, in effect, limited admission to welfare recipients or to those earning little above the welfare subsistence level; improved income means a raise in rent or expulsion from the project. Apartment assignments are made from a central list. A white person refusing an opening in a neighborhood that he knows to be mostly black is usually housed—he has three choices—where he prefers. The lines of segregation have grown very distinct within projects.

Angry Negroes say that a responsible housing authority could have avoided such separateness among the poor. They suggest that a refusal to offer alternatives to applicants rejecting original apartment openings would have done the trick. It seems too simple a solution. Blacks and whites arbitrarily placed in the same building do not automatically become a community. They need to share interests, goals, and purposes before they can begin to communicate with each other. The involvement of black and white tenants in the management and maintenance of their projects may supply a commonality that can perhaps replace the existing mutual distrust.

Certainly, the common interests—in this case,

mostly professional—of the middle and upper-class tenants living in the higher-income public projects or co-ops have provided a meaningful bond between blacks and whites. Integration here is the natural association of people who have something to say to each other.

And the elderly white groups for whom housing has been provided in some of the low-income public projects have had comparatively little difficulty in their associations with a majority black population. They share their pleasures of sitting in the sun, playing a game of checkers, or talking about their grandchildren with blacks and whites. It may be that the symbols and anxieties contributing to black and white divisiveness among other age groups lose some of their importance in later years.

Basically, among white liberals, the symbols and anxieties are relatively few. But they are deep-rooted and impelling. Status is probably the one most meaningful symbol. Housing authorities eager to amend their grievous concrete jungle mistakes have been concentrating in some cities on vest–pocket projects— more or less inconspicuous, average-size buildings placed in better neighborhoods, sometimes near middle or upper-level private housing. In most cases, this has caused a gradual exodus from the luxury apartments. What is the point in paying an absurdly high rental when the neighborhood is becoming poor? Poor, here, usually means black. And as every good status seeker knows, the presence of blacks in a neighborhood can only serve to downgrade the rest of the people who live in it.

Some luxury apartment dwellers flee for other

reasons. They prefer not to look on the face of the poor. It is too distressing an experience. It can also be an offensive one. The poor are not always as quiet or as clean or as tidy as they might be.

They may even be inclined to crime—especially when the temptation of affluent living is within arm's reach, so to speak. Residents in middle-class Negro neighborhoods, usually bordering on lower-class Negro neighborhoods, have for years complained of the robberies and assaults to which they are subjected. Whites often quote this as an acceptable rationale for their own fears. When they are liberal whites, they may add that they are really all for vest pocket housing but, "Please, not right next door!"

If apartment rents continue to skyrocket and the availability of more moderate housing remains limited, white middle and upper-class urban residents may yet learn to live next door and, if not to like the proximity, at least to get used to it. Most of them have already accepted the token Negro who has come more and more frequently to live in their own buildings. He is, of course, so much easier to have around when he is a Sidney Poitier, the one Negro, so it is rumored, in a lavish thirty-five story West side apartment building.

Other factors are, in their ways, also affecting the urban housing patterns of this nation. A Federal program now provides for rent supplements to low-income tenants living in middle-class buildings. It is an alternative to public housing and one way of breaking the black ghetto pattern.

City housing authorities think they have found another in the open space projects they are now planning. These are two-story buildings, separated by small gardens with a bench or two where an adult can relax and with individual play areas for young children. The use of land may not be as economical here as it was in the original slum-based, high-rise projects or even in the vest-pocket programs. But the reduction in population density and the psychological feeling of ownership that the small home and garden are meant to engender may pay off in less property deterioration. The smallness is also intended to encourage greater integration. Whites may not feel themselves quite so overwhelmed or encompassed by blacks in this garden type of enclave and be less fearful about sharing it. Hopefully, a tone of neighborliness will prevail and help both blacks and whites to learn to know each other as people.

Legislatively, things are beginning to look up, too. Two housing bills, stalled in committee at the time of Dr. Martin Luther King's death, got Congressional approval soon after. One provides several hundred million dollars in government money for the financing of mortages on low-income one or two-family homes. The assistance enables average Negro wage earners to do what many middle-class blacks have long been doing—to escape from tokenism and rent exploitation to a home of their own. New Jersey already boasts a development of one-family homes financed in this way. The new development abuts on an older totally black community but its own streets are integrated and the residents seem to enjoy a sense of communal pride.

The other bill desegregates over 90 per cent of the housing in the United States. It exempts only transactions where the owner sells his own house without the services of a broker or discriminatory advertising, rentals in a building of four units or fewer, occupied by the owner—and he, too, must offer his property on the open market—and non-commercial housing owned by a private club or religious organization for the group's own use.

The Supreme Court decision of June 17, 1968 went further when it upheld a civil rights law of 1866 prohibiting race discrimination in the sale and rental of all real estate. Congressional action in passing the 1866 legislation was interpreted by the Court as a means of insuring the freedom that the Thirteenth Amendment gave to the American slave. Justice Potter Stewart, writing the majority opinion, stated: ". . . the Thirteenth Amendment includes the freedom to buy whatever a white man can buy, the right to live wherever a white man can live. If Congress cannot say that being a freeman means at least that much, then the Thirteenth Amendment made a promise that the nation cannot keep."

The Civil Rights Act of 1866 may go far beyond the scope of the Federal Open Housing Law enacted in 1968 but the remedies available for enforcing the old law are weaker. Under the new law, a Negro can obtain a court order against discrimination plus actual damages and punitive damages up to one thousand dollars. Provisions also exist for mediation by the Department of Housing and Urban Development and for the United States Attorney General to bring suit in order to break up a pattern or practice of discrimination. The old law makes provision for court orders barring discrimination but says nothing about money damages and spells out no other means of enforcement. A number of civil rights lawsuits will undoubtedly be testing the strength of the law and of the Supreme Court decision in upholding it.

But what seems to give blacks most reason for optimism is the potential of the new Model Cities Program. It offers a positive means for a comprehensive attack on the urban ghettoes.

Sixty-eight cities, among them Atlanta, Baltimore, Chicago, Philadelphia, and New York have been chosen on the basis of urban need to participate in the Model Cities Program. Cities may supplement Federal aid with their own tax-levied funds.

Federal financing provides each city with a block grant for multi-purpose use. A city can decide on its own priorities for where the money goes and how much is to be spent on which undertaking. The Model Cities Program does not limit changes to building development. A city may believe, for example, that health and sanitation facilities are equally important and direct some of its money to those services. Much innovative thinking has come about as a result of this greater flexibility.

In some cities, Model Cities planning is focusing on the rebuilding of streets, schools, and hospitals, as well as living quarters. In others, it is extending money to existing health, education, welfare, safety, sanitation, and urban renewal programs for the development of supplementary plans. A number of cities are including the open space projects on their drawing boards. A few are considering ideas about buying the privately-owned housing for eventual repurchase by the tenants as cooperatives.

Representatives from the Office of Economic Opportunity and from the Departments of Health, Education, and Welfare, and Housing and Urban Development are meeting with city organizers to expedite all preparatory steps. Approximately two-thirds of the time usually needed for planning and approval is being cut by the coordination of these Federal departments with the appropriate city departments. Construction in the Brownsville area of Brooklyn began in September 1969, only one year after the initiation of the program.

Statutes in the Model Cities Program make mandatory widespread local participation and maximum employment of area residents in all phases of the program. All cities involved have begun to use local communities in these ways.

Organization usually begins with the development of a city-wide Model Cities planning committee. A typical committee includes representatives from city departments and from the community at large. Each geographic area that the Model Cities Program is to cover has its own local planning committee, made up of community representatives and of city department specialists who act as consultants only. The local committee recommends its own director and through the director hires its urban planners, architects, and engineers. The committee also approves—or disapproves—all broad planning. When a committee does not approve, it works with its director for the implementation of its own ideas.

Efforts to employ area residents are concentrating at this stage on the construction aspects of the program. The use of skilled workers here may augur a significant breakthrough in the building trades industries. In one ghetto area, a contract has already been negotiated with the union permitting a percentage of local Negroes to enter the union and to be hired as union members. The prospect of the large number of jobs that a Model Cities program offers undoubtedly influenced the union decision.

As the program develops, local residents will be hired wherever possible to work as plasterers, painters, plumbers, floor layers, window installers, renting agents, maintenance men, etc. The Model Cities Program may indeed be the answer to the black cry for planning that is "ours." With the integrated housing that is anticipated it may finally be a meaningful housing answer for both black and white have–nots. Only two elements of dispute have arisen so far. One is the limited amount of funds, Congress cut the already inadequate appropriation in 1968. The other is the complaint that the increase of tax-exempt construction—for the Model City clinics, hospitals, community centers, etc.—and the leveling of existing tightly-packed housing to create some of the open spaces also anticipated in the program will further shrink the city's already declining property tax base.

No such comforting statement can be made about the Urban Renewal programs which have, in most cases, been controversial from the start. The chief accusation hurled against Urban Renewal is that it has uprooted and dislocated so many disadvantaged groups. Blacks look upon it as "Negro removal." The Department of Housing and Urban Development has recognized this as a fact and begun to rearrange its priorities. Little assistance will be given to projects aimed at creating housing for upper-income levels or at bolstering the economic strength of a neighborhood with industries or office buildings if this means a reduction in the supply of low-cost housing. Maximum support will go to projects that directly assist low-income families in obtaining adequate housing. Urban Renewal is to aim for a balanced community with a strong focus on the needs of low-income groups. There will probably be better opportunities for planning in this direction where Urban Renewal ventures are incorporated into Model City programs.

All the programs and efforts described, however, merely scratch the surface of the over-all picture with its components of a rapidly rising urban Negro population, a tendency on the part of many people to want to live with their kind—which may have little to do with prejudice—and an attitude on the part of just as many—or more—that can only be interpreted as downright prejudice.

From 1960 to 1966, the Negro population of all central cities rose 2.4 million. Natural growth accounted for 1.4 million and in-migration for the rest. It is estimated that it will rise 72 per cent to 20.8 million by 1983, 6 million by natural growth and 2.7 through in-migration. The rate of increase is fastest in the areas where Negro growth has been concentrated in the past two decades. Washington, D.C. and Newark are already more than half Negro. New Orleans and Richmond are expected to become so by 1971, Baltimore and Jacksonville by 1972, and Gary, Indiana, by 1973. What meaning does a projected Federal appropriation of one billion dollars for a

Model Cities Program have in relation to these staggering statistics?

It is important to remember that the natural growth means more dependent children and that the inmigration is usually of blacks from rural areas with few skills that an expanding technological society can utilize. Whites who are not necessarily prejudiced may still prefer to live apart from such an alien atmosphere. When they seek their own kind, it is to the more sophisticated urban dweller that they are referring and this sophisticate may be a black man, as well as a member of their own ethnic background. Many interracial communities attest to this, among them the West Side of Manhattan and Greenwich Village, both East and West, and Sausalito in California.

The actual cores of prejudice are difficult both to reach and to eliminate. The landlord who tells a black man that an apartment he saw advertised is no longer available can not always be proven a liar. When the apartment is subsequently rented to a white householder, the landlord can easily say that this was the person to whom it had been promised. And for one reason or another, the white person will usually confirm the landlord's statement. Urban League workers have lately been trying sandwiching techniques with some success (CORE attempted it a few years ago). A black man told that an apartment has already been rented is immediately followed by a white man; when the white man is advised that the apartment is available, the Negro reappears. Or vice versa, a white man is shown a vacant apartment, is instantly joined by a Negro interested in renting it. The direct confrontation usually shames or floors a landlord into capitulation.

It is a reflection on the spirit of America that such techniques have to be resorted to. But perhaps that is the way all caste systems are broken. Perhaps people have to be forced into modes of behavior as a preliminary step to changes in attitude. The love that can not be legislated may be developed through meaningful interrelationships. At any rate, with urban housing patterns changing the way they are, the people of America will have their chance to find out.

10.
THE INNER
CITY

The inner city has, in its time, been known by many names. In the last quarter of the nineteenth century and the first quarter of the twentieth, it was called the ghetto. It was then occupied—simultaneously, separately, or in turn, depending on its location—by the Irish, the Jews from Eastern Europe, the Italians, and the Poles. They shared hardships, misery, poverty, crowding, filth, and uncertainty in what came to be known as a slum. As these aliens moved up the economic and social ladder and out into better neighborhoods, the blacks—and later, the Puerto Ricans—moved in. Negroes began to congregate in urban slum areas in the middle 1940's, during and after the war that brought most of them into the cities looking for work. They remained in the slums, extending them, actually, as a rising black population spread out into one fringe area after another. It was usually the black man with a slightly higher income who managed to make this move. But the white man, his own standard of living going up too, moved just as quickly out of successive fringe neighborhoods.

The slum is easily identified, whether it exists as a small geographic section, surrounded by *other* population or, as is more prevalent today, as an area which is crowding the *other* groups out of the metropolis. It is predominantly black; its per capita income is low and the general life style is definitely lower class. Sociologists and educators called it a culturally deprived neighborhood for a while. Then residents began to object, saying they were not at all deprived in terms of their own culture, and disadvantaged community came into favor. Core city, central city, and inner city are the more popular usages. Fifty major cities in the United States have these inner cities.

The meticulousness that has gone into the nomenclature for the slums has not been paralleled by any such care in a consideration of remedies for its ills. It is obviously much easier to talk about the problems than to work out solutions.

For the most part, the suggested solutions have been what Roy Innis calls bandaids. If he means by this that they cover up the wound—and keep it, hopefully, out of sight—without treating the cause, there are numerous instances to support his opinion. The most appealing, perhaps, to the culture-conscious white middle class have been the free summer concerts and theatricals—even Shakespeare—presented on the streets of the ghetto. Clean-up campaigns, in their various versions as carried out in different cities, have many white devotees, too. They find it all very heartening when the television cameras flash the pictures of the covered garbage pail parades or of the slum tenants getting together to beautify a particular block or of the concerned young suburbanites who come out of their retreats to pitch in with paint brushes and geranium seeds for fresh, new window boxes.

That such bright projects do not—and cannot—cure the ills of a sprawling, decaying urban slum may temporarily elude the consciousness of the lulled television viewer. The fact does not frequently escape the attention of aware city officials. But if it is not apathy or indifference that keeps them from more relevant efforts, it is usually a misdirection of available funds or complaints about the need for more money.

Population shifts have left most urban areas with a declining tax base; the more affluent citizens have fled before the invasion of the ghetto. The middle class migration spreads farther and farther from the city core; eventually the majority settle in a suburb—secure, they hope, from the spreading ghetto. As commuters, they pay little or no city taxes. That burden falls on those least able to pay, the poor of the inner cities plus, of course, the comparatively few—and largely resentful—middle and upper-income families who still live in the metropolitan area.

The exploding population of the inner city requires massive expenditures for the public services on which a poor community wholly depends: free health services, hospitals, police protection, fire protection, sanitation, sewage disposal, water supply, parks, playgrounds, and education. The rich do not usually congregate in such numbers as the poor do in their tenements or slum-based projects. The rich can also afford private schools, private medical care, summer camps for their children, buildings which are fireproof, and garbage disposal units which reduce the problems of sanitation.

Salaries for all employes in public service have gone up, making the city bill higher. And it will grow higher still if the city is to meet the demands for improved services that an aroused black ghetto now demands.

Some few economies could probably be achieved by the poor themselves. Better care of project property, for example, would reduce the cost of housing deterioration. A better response to the pleas for the use of litter baskets might ease some of the problems of sanitation. But the ghetto does not usually heed "establishment" admonitions. It sees things from another point of view altogether. The projects, with all their regulations and inspections, belong to the establishment, not to the tenants. The streets are never properly cleaned, to begin with. An extra bit of trash— or even a bag full of garbage thrown from a window —will not make much difference. If cooperation is ever to be secured from an embittered inner city, it will come as a result of the ghetto residents' own involvement. For that, local leadership needs to be encouraged and made durable.

Indigenous leadership has often accomplished what a ghetto believed impossible. Some inner city clinics are now staying open until midnight to relieve overcrowding. More ghetto hospitals are in the process of construction. They are gradually being attached to fine medical schools. Neighborhood health service centers and medical societies affiliated with local hospitals are being developed. In one inner city, a council made up mainly of residents who are entitled to local health services has been set up. It interprets patient reactions and their suggestions for improvements to clinics and hospitals, works to influence the manner in which services are offered, and helps to dispel the medical mystique for the community. As yet, the American Medical Association has offered no comment about this cooperative local involvement.

And black leaders have certainly made their point about the feelings of a black community toward a white police force. Resentment is exacerbated in cities such as Baltimore, where there are more white cops from outside the city limits on the force than black cops from inside. In most inner cities, black police are now being added to this "army of occupation" to make it more representative of a city-involved service. If the black leaders can also achieve the delivery of better sanitation services, they may succeed in using that psychological impetus for motivating local educational programs to help keep neighborhoods clean.

But black leadership, like the white population, keeps moving out of the ghetto—although not for the same reasons. To maintain their positions, leaders need to deliver to their followers. Black leaders get tired of pleading with the establishment for pittances which do little to halt the steady deterioration of the ghetto. After a while, they, too, become uninvolved and move on to live more pleasantly elsewhere. The ghetto remains.

It is, however, comforting to know that even the pittance programs are well planned, today. They involve community thinking which is not likely to come up with such "wholesale" conceptions as the multistory, low-income projects. The demands that crowded populations make on local schools, hospitals, clinics, and welfare departments are anticipated by a community that lives with such services.

Consumer education is one of the small programs that is making steady headway in a number of inner cities. It is teaching some residents the facts of economic life and all of them how to protect themselves against economic exploitation.

In a democratic capitalist society, the customer must always be a source of some profit to the seller. But profit borders on fraud when food prices go up on Welfare check day, when small shops extending credit between checks pad the notations "in the book," and when chain food stores sell the rejects— and at higher prices—from better neighborhoods in their ghetto branches. Buying on time or loan contracts with small-print clauses, which sometimes charge customers almost as much in interest as the original purchase price or loan, are legion. The profit statements of stores and loan companies do not show the need to up prices or interest, as is sometimes claimed, to compensate for shoplifting or defaulting on payments.

The consumer education programs that are most successful are those that truly educate. Classes are now being conducted, not merely to advise inner city residents to examine their contracts carefully, but to teach them how to read all of the clauses. These classes also give instruction in comparative shopping and in the use of consumer reports.

Other classes teach welfare recipients how to make appetizing dishes out of the dull surplus foods that they are entitled to. Many housewives have admitted that they did not use some of these foods before. There just didn't seem to be anything good to do with them.

To help solve the problem of deceptive loan contracts or exorbitant interest rates, some inner cities have established their own credit unions. Members pay small sums into them weekly, gradually amassing a collateral against which to borrow. Loans are extended beyond the actual collateral—or even without it—when the need exists.

Perhaps the most innovative of the consumer education programs have been the cooperative buying clubs. Members meet once a week or more to list the meat, milk, eggs, bread, fruit, and vegetables that they want. A committee buys the food from distributors and resells it at a trifle above cost to the consumers involved.

Another small program that is proving successful is the removal by private contractors of abandoned cars from cluttered ghetto streets. In New York City, approximately six hundred of them are being removed each week. It is anticipated that thirty-six thousand will be off the streets by the end of a year. This may seem a piddling sort of project to outer-city residents. To the dense inner city, it is highly important. Ghetto children use the cars as their playgrounds, cutting themselves on broken window glass and getting caught in the fires which they like to light in the dark, mysterious interiors. Ambulances and fire trucks are impeded by the congestion caused by abandoned cars. Delays very often mean a loss of lives.

Most inner cities have been clamoring for this kind of removal for years. Very often sanitation departments have made promises and have eventually hauled a few cars away. The private contractors, on the other hand, have moved with a speed and efficiency that has led many students of inner-city problems to speculate about the advantages of by-passing city departments where urgent inner-city services are concerned.

In the opinion of many inner-city residents, most services would be more successfully handled if they were locally controlled. The feeling is that the services would be more responsive to community interests and structure if there were not such a distance between them, if residents could communicate with the persons directly accountable instead of with an impersonal bureaucracy. Local Urban Action Task Forces and the Community Corporations which carry out local anti-poverty programs already provide community linkage for inner-city services. The next step, they argue, is decentralization to extend the linkage to actual community control.

But these are only ideas for implementation of existing services to the inner city. If they are ever going to have any meaningful effect on the urban Negro ghetto, money is needed to expand their efforts. A still greater expenditure is required if the living conditions of the average ghetto black is to be brought close to that of the average white. And that is one of the principal thrusts of the black revolution.

The black revolutionary does not particularly care where the money is to come from to make his streets as clean as the white man's or his housing as comfortable or his medical care as complete or as convenient. If he stops to think about the cost at all, it is in terms of the white man's historic debt to him: a white society made him dependent; a white society has to pay for it.

City mayors and managers may agree with this concept, or they may believe that meeting the demands is less costly than repairing the effects of urban riots, or they may simply feel that no just society can ignore the needs of its poor, even when these needs reflect more and more the rising expectations engendered by a constantly higher national living standard. But whatever their opinions, they must think about money.

Much consideration has been given to the prospect of luring private capital investment into ghetto areas. For the most part, white-dominated firms and industries have resisted. They believe the risks and costs are too great. Business insurance is especially expensive in inner cities. And with the ever-present danger of riots, even this costly protection is being refused in many cases. Private investors who have been involved are beginning to withdraw their capital. Tax incentives such as a Federal write-off for losses incurred during a riot may persuade some of them to change their minds or induce others to try.

There has been much talk and some planning about the establishment of government buildings in ghetto areas to house, for example, Federal Selective Service offices or Federal regional offices of Health, Education, and Welfare or of Housing and Urban Develop-

ment, state income tax or motor vehicle offices, various city departments, and even city courts. The presence of middle-class civil service workers and upper-
level executives, both black and white, would stimulate trade and the creation of new businesses to
serve them, such as banks, department stores, spe-
cialty clothing shops, book stores, drugstores, good
restaurants, coffee shops, stationery stores, beauty
parlors, etc. The daily personal contacts could help
to reduce fears and encourage understanding and
communication.

The greatest resource for economic aid, however, is
still the Federal government. Under conditions of
steady economic growth—and the American economy
has been consistently productive—the fiscal dividends
from the Federal revenue system range from eleven
billion dollars to fourteen billion dollars per year.
The tax surcharge adds approximately another ten
billion dollars annually. It is probable that all large
cities containing a high proportion of low-income
Negroes in deteriorating core areas will attempt to
draw on this resource for the substantial assistance
they need.

Undoubtedly, there will be competing demands
on Federal revenues. The feeling of the inner city
is that its only real hope for significant financial help
from the Federal government lies in the political
strength it can organize. Toward this aim, Negro
leaders have been working to eliminate gerrymandering and to promote political reapportionment.

Gerrymandering has always meant the drawing of
election district lines to favor one religious or ethnic
or political group over another. Its effect on the

Negro ghetto has been one of diffusion. The natural boundary of the inner city has been ignored and pieces of it have been chopped off to attach to other election districts. These were always white. A black citizen in the attached section had only white alternative candidates to vote for and, in his disillusioned opinion, white candidates did not give much thought to the needs of blacks in what might ideally have been hoped for in an "American All" democracy. Wherever gerrymandering has been halted, black candidates have appeared on the slate. Bedford-Stuyvesant in Brooklyn elected its first Negro Member of Congress, Shirley Chisholm, in November 1968.

Political reapportionment makes population the basis for the number of candidates to which an election district is entitled. Without reapportionment, a district including only five thousand people has the same number of representatives as a district with twenty-five thousand. The democratic benefits to a heavily populated inner city are self-evident. Negroes hope to accomplish much through an improved system of political reapportionment.

Of necessity, their principal concern will probably be with the inner city. This is where roughly 89 per cent of the total national growth of the Negro population is concentrated. This is where the black man lives with continuous poverty, segregation, and inequality of opportunity.

11.
GET
WHITEY!

Few black men are persuaded that a white society has their interests at heart. Suspicions nurtured by centuries of indifference are only aggravated when a Congress moves with characteristic slowness to put social change into motion. When urban bureaucracies, working within the democratic system, place obstacles in the way of immediate action, the black man's first impulse is to take matters into his own hands. He has recently threatened, for example, to burn unoccupied ghetto buildings, frequented by drug addicts, sex perverts, and unsuspecting children, if they are not boarded up (cost, approximately two hundred dollars per building). The system requires formal proceedings expected to take at least six months and to cost thousands of dollars in man hours. Black restiveness can no longer tolerate such delays. The mood is one of urgency, intensified, perhaps, by the feelings of triumph about advances so far achieved. According to the final report of the President's "Riot Commission," a growing majority of the black population now thinks of riots as an acceptable form of social protest. A militant few are evidently rejecting even the riot as inadequate. The deliberate shootings in Gary, Cleveland, and New York seem to indicate that some blacks believe only the tactics of actual guerrilla warfare will sufficiently frighten Whitey into speeding up his delivery to the Negro.

For the black man, Whitey is always the figure of oppression. The symbolization may take various forms, however. In the ghetto, Whitey is frequently the Jew. It is, of course, ironic that the Jew should be thus singled out, for he has been in the conspicuous forefront of movements intended to help the American Negro. Jewish organizations, planned originally to secure fair employment, education, and renting practices for their own people, continued to push for these policies when Jewish self-interest was no longer involved. Jewish money and membership supported the CORE organization when it was founded in 1942 and for many years afterward. Jewish groups played a major role in organizing the New York State Committee Against Discrimination in Housing after the failure of court action to change the anti-Negro policies of a life insurance company housing development. Black leaders are well aware of this commitment. But black leaders prefer, as they put it, not to let the Jew off the hook. The liberal Jew, they say, pointing the accusing finger, did nothing to restrain the exploitation of the Negro by the "other" Jew.

The other Jew is largely the ghetto storekeeper or landlord who seems, for most ghetto residents, to be about the only non-official white person they meet. All of the envy and hatred and resentment meant for the white man are therefore vented against his representative in the ghetto, the Jew. As a shopkeeper, he is criticized for overcharging, for making his money in the ghetto, and since he does not live there, for taking all the cash out with him. As a landlord, he is attacked for his exorbitant rentals, his uncaring neglect of building needs, and his usual absenteeism. It does no good to argue that a storekeeper's chief interest is to make money, no matter how and as long as he can get away with it, that many store owners, Jewish or non-Jewish, live far away from their places of business located in residential communities in and outside of the ghetto, and that landlords, Jewish or otherwise, are notorious for their efforts to exploit tenants. The Jew remains *the* shopkeeper and *the* landlord that the black man encounters in the ghetto and in the fringe Jewish neighborhoods that he expands into. And the Jew, in the minds of black leadership, is apparently expected to know better. Perhaps he should. He, too, is a minority with a background of persecution. But on the other hand, as blacks are quick to counter when more is demanded of them than their history enables them to be, Negroes—except for the Black Muslims —do not assume that they are superior human beings. Evidently, liberal Jews do not make that assumption about other Jews, either.

There are still other Jews with whom the Negro comes into conflict. There is the middle-class

Jewish housewife who is resented because of her position of authority in the master-servant relationship. There is the Jewish professional who preceded the black man into government service so that he is now the principal, for example, with the new Negro teacher serving under him. There is the Jewish union—Jewish in the sense that Jews struggled to organize it and Jews still hold top union positions—with memberships that are now mostly Negro and Puerto Rican. Neither group is particularly happy about the Jews on the union payroll. And there is the Jewish political leader with his consistently excellent record on civil rights and other relevant issues. But the neighborhood he has been representing is now Negro-dominated and aspiring black leaders would like and intend to get all such political positions for themselves.

If only because he so frequently has just made it into the place or rank or neighborhood where the black man wants to go, this other Jew is resented by the Negro. The relationship between inferior and superior is especially hard to bear when the superior position is barely beyond the reach of the man whom society labels inferior and who feels himself inferior. It is no wonder then that the average Jew, despite his long tradition of liberalism, today fears the black revolution. He can not help but see it as a movement with growing anti-Semitic leanings.

But it is not against the Jew that the black man directs his most violent angers. Those he reserves for the policeman, Jew or Gentile, who typifies for him the "compleat" Whitey. Most urban officials have become aware, if belatedly, of the tensions that the

presence of white police in a black ghetto neighborhood can produce. City mayors and managers have
augmented their police departments with black patrolmen, black sergeants, even black deputy inspec-
tors. They have developed task forces and crowd control groups and rumor control units and community
patrols and tactical patrols and forces and patrols
by many other names but similarly planned to handle
ghetto riots. All of these men are trained in the new
police philosophy of staying attuned to the sensitivities of a ghetto, of avoiding overreactions that can
create an incident, and of containing individual disorders so that they do not erupt into widespread
riots. Many are also intensively trained in the specialized military techniques of riot control. The black
nationalist splinter groups so eager for black-white
confrontation may not realize what they are letting
themselves in for when they really put Whitey to the
test.

Their own techniques have so far been simple and
predictable. They perform some act which provokes
an edgy white policeman to overrespond with a
hasty arrest, a flash of his gun, or even a shot from
the gun. A riot almost inevitably follows.

So far, the white man has shown restraint in his use
of retaliatory force. Even in Cleveland, where the
shooting of the three white policemen was allegedly
murder, coldly calculated to provoke confrontation,
no reactive white violence ensued. And the National
Guard was not called in until black community leaders said that they wanted this help.

No one is completely sure—although there are
some very educated guesses—as to whether the black

invitations to open confrontation are the acts of isolated extremists or the organized strategy of one or more black nationalist organizations. There is uncertainty, too, about the future targets of the new black activists. Frantz Fanon and Regis Debray, their revolutionary philosophers are not content to see blacks act out their rebellion in the destruction of their own communities. "Burn, Baby, Burn," the song with the mournful refrain, "When I burn myself out of the ghetto, I burn my own self up," may no longer be expressing the black revolutionary mood. "Get Whitey!" seems to be taking its place.

Whites comfort themselves with the knowledge that the number of extremists is still small. The black plotters involved in the Cleveland provocation totaled forty. Seven blacks were killed along with the three white policemen and one white bystander.

But comfort notwithstanding, they are going ahead with plans to meet black terrorism. Official preparations on the part of the white army—and it may as well be called that, for the planning on both black and white sides seems more and more to resemble preparation for a war—fall into three categories: weapons, tactics, and the use of intelligence channels. All are being organized with that terrifying efficiency America can muster when it rallies to meet an emergency.

Weapons for police and riot squads are now actual instruments of war. At the 1967 meeting of the International Association of Chiefs of Police, armored personnel cars were prominently displayed in the exhibit area. Detroit has stated that its current anti-riot equipment includes armored vests, machine guns, and battle cars. Cambridge, Maryland used CS, the military training gas which adds a sense of suffocation to the effects of CN, the ordinary tear gas, to quell its disorders. MACE, the paralyzing gas is being bought by city police departments throughout the country. Hand grenades, bazookas, recoilless rifles, shotguns, submachine guns, gas masks, riot helmets, and riot batons are becoming standard equipment.

Tactics for dealing with disorders are no longer haphazard. They are now as carefully and strategically planned as a battle, even a campaign. All major American cities are mapped for defense with plans drawn —by the city and state police departments, the city fire departments, the state disaster headquarters, and National Guard units—for command centers, food centers, food sources, and areas ringed for containment of ghetto residents. The classic military advantage of controlling the heights has not been overlooked. Plans include the placement of armed men on rooftops by helicopter. Philadelphia already has men learning how to shoot from ladders, rooftops, and from helicopters, too. In anticipation of extended chemical warfare, special teams are being trained in the utilization of various gases and other chemicals, including liquid banana peel, the slippery chemical. Communications problems are solved by the use of a single emergency radio band, as in Illinois, where the statewide band now replaces the separate radio bands formerly assigned to city police, county police, fire departments, and the National Guard. Anti-sniper teams, and in New York, members of the Police Department, are equipped with walkie-talkies. Morale has been studied and the suggestion made for the use of a bullhorn to give the front line a sense of solidarity with the unit behind. Buses are available to move arrestees quickly out of their own neighborhoods and into armories or other large centers where they can be arraigned far from their local police station which, it is feared, could become the target for further attacks. Experienced former district attorneys and clerical personnel are on hand at these centers to do the required processing. No detail seems to be neglected in all this careful preparation. Even the United States Army is ready. General Harold K. Johnson, Army Chief of Staff, has testified that the active Army has seven task forces, each of brigade size, specifically earmarked and available for civil disturbance duty.

The information about the painstaking use of intelligence is still more impressive. If the situation were not so terribly real, the maneuverings in this area might be amusingly reminiscent of a grade B spy movie. Local intelligence work is now principally devoted to riots and civil rights movements. Agents are planted to infiltrate suspect organizations. The Justice Department has recommended a computer bank of information on ringleaders. A central intelligence net may one day link existing connections among agitators in various parts of the nation. At the moment, local daily charts report the comings and goings of militant leaders, the dates of their anticipated meetings, and the supposed hiding places of secret weapons. Intelligence reports of this kind led to the arrests in New York and Philadelphia of the members of RAM—the Revolutionary Action Movement—who were charged with possessing arsenals and plotting assassinations. In August 1968, Chicago police arrested a group of militant black extremists who were alleged to be plotting the assassination of the two major Democratic Presidential nominees and the simultaneous bombing of seven Chicago police stations.

Black extremists, apprised of all this preparation, usually remain calm. They have their own ideas and programs. They are particularly fond of saying that it took very few men and weapons to fire "the shot heard 'round the world" at the Battle of Bunker Hill. At the same time, they are openly collecting weapons. H. Rap Brown's appeal, "If you can't give a gun, then give a dollar to somebody who can buy a gun," was quoted in the national press. Bazookas and mortars are available to militants as well as to police and can be stored in readiness together with stolen rifles and prepared Molotov cocktails. Leaders who boast that they have studied Che Guevara's guerrilla techniques can pass these along to others. Courses are now being given in countering police moves with clubs, in maneuvering picket signs as shields, in the wearing of defense clothing, including gas masks, in the reading of topographical battle maps and aerial photographs, and in the diverse uses that can be made of rope, knives, flashlights, rocks, bottles, cans, bats, chains, metal pipes, and sharp razor blades. Most of all, extremists feel confident because they believe time is on their side. More and more whites are leaving the cities daily. Soon the cities will be ramparts of blacks. They will elect their own officers, run their own governments. Whites will no longer be dealing with the seat of city government from positions of authority and majority. They will then be coming to the blacks for favorable policy decisions and for services to meet their needs.

What the black extremist militants are not counting on is the stubborness of the white citizens in preventing any such takeover. Black rioting is still—despite the agitations of the Fanon and Debray disciples— confined to ghetto neighborhoods. And white citizens are resolved that even these must be successfully and permanently stopped. They are voting for larger and larger budgets to enable the purchase by city police departments of more and more effective anti-riot weapons. They declare themselves ready to take up arms. In Newark, white men patrolled their neighborhoods with shotguns. In Detroit, a joint statement prepared by the Citizens Committee for Civil Defense, the Police and Firemen Association for Public Safety, the Chaldean Committee for Preservation of Liberty, the United War Veterans for Defense of the United States Constitution, the American Legion, Post #375, and Breakthrough, the local anti-Negro organization, asked the white populace: "Are you ready now to prepare yourself for the next time? Or will you be forced to stand helplessly by because you were unprepared to defend your home or neighborhood against bands of armed terrorists who will murder the men and rape the women?" To assure the preparation for "next time," Breakthrough provides opportunities for members of the National Rifle Association to teach and demonstrate the use of different types of guns.

These impassioned responses are not limited to the reactionary or lunatic fringe elements in American society. Plain middle-of-the-roaders are making similar decisions that grow out of fear or the wish to protect themselves from looters, vandals, and unruly demonstrators. Kansas City police are training white merchants to use rifles and pistols. White firemen and bus drivers are asking for permission to carry arms. White housewives in middle-class homes are taking combat shooting lessons. Regular classes have been established for them outside of Detroit. Extremist blacks have told their followers: "The gun is an extension of your hand." They probably did not anticipate that it would also become suburbia's new tranquilizer.

White feelings about law enforcement—and some of the crimes in the streets seem deliberately to mock the law—have also become more determined. When Mayor Daley went before the Chicago City Council to ask for additional police so that he could start a crackdown on crime, the Council applauded. The Council floorleader advised him, "We are providing seven hundred policemen commencing next week. If it requires seven thousand or seventy thousand more—whatever necessary—I back your statement to the hilt." In Newark, an irate civilian group stated that it would proceed to take over the duties of the Police Department if police did not change their practice of being so "easy" on the blacks and announced that members were already studying Karate. In New York City, the Policemen's Benevolent Association, speaking for twenty-nine thousand members, declared its intention of enforcing the law "one hundred per cent." The police complained that they had been restrained—"handcuffed" was the way they phrased it—from making arrests by orders advising them not to rock the boat. They felt themselves duty-bound to halt violations of the law.

The President's Commission on Civil Disorders summed the situation up very accurately when it stated that the true source of police strength in maintaining order lies in the respect and good will of the people they serve. At the current stage of the black-white confrontation, the only kind of police force that can control the looting and the disorders is probably one that the black people believe is on their side. Certainly, most of them would approve of efforts made to reduce the muggings that are becoming almost daily occurrences on urban streets. The mayor of the City of New York tried to give the police Whitey this image of patience and understanding and sympathy for Negro outburst. Evidently he failed. White police are obviously chafing under the "handcuffs"—partly because of their own hostilities and partly in response to white complaints. And blacks, continuing to test them, have presumably gone too far.

The eventual solution may be a totally black police force for black ghetto areas. Empathy would then be unstrained. It is encouraging to note that seventy out of the eighty blacks recently graduated from the New York City Police Academy volunteered to serve in the Tactical Patrol Force, the special group organized to enter a troubled area on call and to come down hard with law enforcement. It is also significant that the recruitment of blacks for city police departments has been a slow and difficult process. Many blacks have conflicts about joining the "enemy" ranks. In the black urban ghetto, the policeman is the suburbanite, the symbol of the power structure that exists to attack, not to serve the black man.

But the New York City mayor—and he stated that the Police Commissioner, not the Patrolmen's Benevolent Association, gave the orders in his department—is not likely to give up. Neither will other officials with concern and insight. They may not succeed in overcoming the black man's resentment of his various Whiteys. They will probably make little, if any, headway against black extremist resolve for confrontation. But by minimizing distrust in the white man's intentions, they may undercut support for extremist leadership. While the wheels of democracy grind slowly to extend full equality to the black man, the effort, may at least, stop some of the burning.

12.
THE
BLACK
BLOC

The battle for full equality for the black man in America is being fought in differing ways by the various factions of black society involved in it. Black moderate militants undoubtedly identify with the emotions of the black ghetto rioter. They may even agree with Frantz Fanon, the revolutionary, that violence, when practiced by the wretched and oppressed, can be intrinsically valuable as an assertion of self and as a reversal of the previous act of violence—slavery—which caused the self to be denied. But they do not accept violence as a tactic to which the black revolution must be committed.

Their reluctance in this respect is based on at least two considerations. The first is probably the very practical acknowledgment that the black man can not win in a black-white confrontation which is essentially a contest in violence. A benumbed white nation —too surprised even to believe in a revolt on the part of its subjugated blacks—allowed the black "victories" to pile up: more than one hundred cities wracked by violence since 1964, property damage running to hundreds of millions, and a loss in Negro lives that no one has bothered to count accurately; it has been admitted that large numbers of unidentified blacks, evidently as unknown in death as in life, may never have made it out of the burning buildings. But the shock has worn off. A white society is prepared to fight fire with fire. And there is really no question about who can light the larger conflagration.

The second consideration relates to definitions of black power. In the fluid black revolutionary movement, and in the rhetoric of black revolutionaries, the means and the end are sometimes confused and the exhilaration of illusory strengths may tend to obscure the more meaningful issue. It is indeed true that the goals of black power can be served by the development of a sense of pride and dignity about blackness, as they may also be advanced by the exclusion of whites from civil rights organizations where blacks want to be their own decision-makers. But surely these are steps in the process and not synonymous with black power in any larger sense. And unpremeditated acts of violence against the white man and or his property, cathartic as these expressions of hatred—or of selfhood—may prove, cannot be equated with any significant meaning of black power. Ironically, it is the moderate militants who reject such extremist concepts of black power as not sufficiently far-reaching. They also dismiss as unrealistic—and occasionally, as nihilistic—the extremist proposals which define black power in terms of a totally separate black state.

What black moderate militants are opting for is the use of pressure-group tactics in the historical tradition of the American political process. They are cognizant of the white man's resistance to the actualities of full black equality. But in accordance with black revolutionary strategy, they intend to make their demands from a position of strength. For them, black power lies, as power does basically in any democracy, in the political advantage.

Blacks are probably the biggest special interest group in American politics today. The impact of their vote as a bloc can swing a national election. A Presidential election is sometimes carried by a two to three per cent vote. John F. Kennedy owed his victory to one of the slimmest margins in history: 51 per cent in his favor as against 49 per cent for Richard Nixon. It is known that Negroes provided Kennedy's victory margin in several key states. They nearly made it for Hubert Humphrey, too, 80 per cent or more in most ghettoes choosing him as their presidential candidate in 1968 and reducing Nixon's victory to a plurality of 118,000 votes.

The two major political parties are well aware of this power. But any attempt on their part to court the black vote must be undertaken with caution. Their actions may be interpreted as a concession to blacks and cost them more white votes than they can win among Negroes. White candidates wooing the vote on the state-wide scene are equally careful to avoid a black-white polarization. When they are shrewd, they manage to avert both backlash and blacklash. Ronald Reagan, running for the governorship of California, never said a word directly against Negroes. He simply emphasized the need for law and order and denounced the mothers of out-of-wedlock children who receive public assistance funds. Obviously, enough citizens, black and white, agreed with him to vote him into office. The same may perhaps be said about the Nixon victory. He, too, stressed law and order in his campaign.

In these sensitive times, an open anti-black position may be equally fragmenting in its effects on a party or its candidate. Moderate whites can also ally themselves with blacks in a common revolt. They joined forces to defeat George P. Mahoney, the Democratic candidate for Governor of Maryland in 1966, when he made a racist issue out of open housing.

There is certainly precedent for Negro bloc-voting —even excepting the original loyalty to the party of Abraham Lincoln. Masses of blacks moved away from this historic allegiance to vote for Franklin Delano Roosevelt and his economic and welfare projects. Almost all voted the Democratic ticket against Barry Goldwater and what he proposed as economic and social programs. And many are voting with ever greater sophistication about where their own interests lie. Blacks gave 90 per cent of their vote to moderate William B. Spong Jr., running in 1966 as a Democrat for a Virginia Senate seat and less than 20 per cent to the Democratic Southern conservative, Harry Byrd Jr., running for the other Senate seat. They voted 85 per cent in 1966, for Edward R. Brooke, a Republican Negro candidate for the Senate from Massachusetts but split their ticket to give John Volpe, his Republican running mate for Governor, less than 40 per cent of their vote. In the November 1968 election, nine black Congressional Representatives—Shirley Chisholm of Brooklyn, New York; William L. Clay of St. Louis, Missouri; Louis Stokes of Cleveland, Ohio; Adam Clayton Powell of Harlem, New York; Charles Diggs and John Conyers of Detroit; William Dawson of Chicago; Robert Nix of Philadelphia; and Augustus Hawkins of Los Angeles—were elected to the House. Three of these are newly–elected members; all are Democrats. In North Carolina, Henry Frye was elected to the 170-member General Assembly which has been all white for the last seventy years. In Florida, Joe Kershaw became the first black citizen to take office in the state's lower chamber in more than ninety–six years. There are now twelve black representatives and two black senators in the Georgia legislature, six black House members and two black senators in the Tennessee state government, two black representatives and one black senator in the state government in Texas, and one black representative in the Virginia, Louisiana, and Mississippi legislatures.

Blacks have naturally moved toward parties and candidates committed to liberal reform. They may no longer be able to rely, however, on movements that have been traditionally liberal. The Democratic party now includes not only the old-time white supremacist Southerner but also the new Northern ethnic white separatist. This white separatist is usually a member of the working class who takes pride in his liberal or democratic affiliations. But as a lower or lower middle-income earner, he lives closer to the inner city and faces the greater menace from Negro rioting and city crime. He is also more inclined to view fair employment practices as a threat to his own chances for new jobs or promotions. And in-busing affects his children more than it does the lives of those who attend private schools or the publicly-supported schools in or near the suburbs. The support of George Wallace as the Presidential candidate of the American Independent party came largely from such citizens, both above and below the Mason-Dixon line. They shared his rage about the money government and foundations were pouring into experimental projects that, in their opinion, might eventually abolish Civil Service or other established government programs and their own jobs simultaneously. And they loved his formula, accompanied by the appropriate gesture with an imaginary shotgun, for the control of rioters: "Bam! Bam! Shoot 'em dead!" White liberal principles evidently go out the window when black interests impinge on working-class security.

Organized labor seems to reflect this primary drive for self–protection. On the whole, unions have neither fostered good race relations nor gone along with membership plans that would help meet the employment needs of the cities. Actually, big business, the traditional enemy of working-class reform, has lately shown itself at least as liberal in its hiring and training practices. The customary allegiances are in evidence when big business opposes price freezes and unions fight wage controls proposed to help curb inflation. But the line-ups turn confusing again when labor remains conservative about Vietnam and both labor and big business disapprove of the costs of public assistance. Blacks will undoubtedly have to play it by ear when they begin seriously to exert their pressure as a bloc.

They have not even begun to realize their potential in this regard. Nowhere near all eligible black citizens are voting. Some are still not registered to vote. And many registered voters are not putting in an appearance at the polls. A sense of deep futility keeps them from participating in what seems to be an empty ritual.

Their feelings are unfortunately justified. White candidates elected to public office have usually shown little or no concern about the black community. Even Negro candidates whom blacks have hopefully voted for have not always been reseponsive to their needs. Only a few of those currently holding fairly high political positions are what they call black blacks.

Senator Brooke from Massachusetts—the first black senator in America since Reconstruction—is conceded by most blacks to be a white Negro. He is not from the ghetto and does not sufficiently identify himself with its interests to represent ghetto blacks. He has, as they sometimes put it, anesthetized himself into believing that he is above the color line. His record on civil rights is undoubtedly good but civil rights are not the core of his concern. He moves in a white world and is not likely to exercise the kind of leadership that would give the United States Senate a keener consciousness of black ghetto problems.

William Dawson, Congressman from Chicago for the last twenty-six years, is sometimes classified by the ghetto as a trader. He gives it handouts to keep tempers cool. At no time do ghetto blacks see him as their delegate to the white structure. The representation is the other way around. He comes as a messenger from the white structure to explain away its various omissions and procrastinations. He has always been a machine politician and is not expected to change.

Charles Diggs, Congressman from Detroit, is another party machine man. Ghetto black needs have not particularly affected his career. And during the fourteen years that he has been in office, he has made little impression on the black ghetto. Congressman Conyers, also from Detroit, reflects much the same image.

Another United States Negro Congressman is much better known. He is Adam Clayton Powell from New York, beloved by ghetto blacks as their "rabbi"—the soul brother who interceded, spoke, and "delivered" for them—and viewed by them as the only black official on a national level whom the structure has not been able to cut down to size. He not only represented the black community in Congress; he demanded from Congress a peer-level relationship. As chairman of the Education and Labor Committee, he held a highly influential post. In the opinion of the black community, it was basically his refusal to be humble and subservient that roused the House Ethics Committee from its usual dormancy—to expel Powell. He has since returned, though without seniority.

The November 1967 election gave the Negroes two black mayors: Carl B. Stokes in Cleveland and Richard G. Hatcher in Gary, both Democrats. The vast majority of their votes came from Negroes. At least 98,000 of Stokes' 129,398 votes appear to have come from members of his own race. It is estimated that Negroes account for an even higher percentage of Hatcher's 39,330 vote.

It is also estimated that, in both instances, white Democrats bolted the party in droves because they did not want to vote for a black man. In Cleveland, Seth C. Taft, Republican nephew of "Mr. Republican," the late Senator Taft, polled 127,717 votes—this in a city that has for years been a Democratic stronghold. An analysis has shown that most of these votes came from the white working-class wards, long considered the backbone of the city's Democratic organization. In Gary, Hatcher's own party deserted him after he won the primaries. Whole precincts left the Democratic fold and brought Joseph B. Radigan, a Republican, within 1,400 votes of victory—again in a Democratic city, this time one which had been unalterably Democratic since the F.D.R. era.

So far, Stokes and Hatcher have been both responsive to total city needs and sensitive to the particular problems of the black community. Hatcher is just beginning to sort out the problems in Gary. Stokes has started to move toward some structure in providing better programs and services to the Cleveland ghetto.

A third Negro mayor, Walter Washington of the District of Columbia, was, as the law requires, appointed to his post by the President. He knows the ghetto and understands its problems. But according to the ghetto, he doesn't push for delivery. Ghetto blacks attribute his non-militancy largely to a conflict of loyalties and are agitating for future mayors of Washington, D.C. to be elected by the people.

The majority of Negro political figures do not rise to prominence on the basis of mass support from ghetto blacks. Genuine black representatives are beginning to emerge but most are still selected by white political leadership and subtly, or otherwise, subjected to white control. Since only thirty per cent of the blacks in the ghettos are registered voters, this is an inevitable pattern. Only the ghetto blacks will put black blacks into office.

And only the black representative who has behind him the loyalty and full support of his constituents will have enough strength to bargain with white party leaders. Negroes in the United States have in the political arena, as well as elsewhere, been traditionally manipulated. Bargaining strength for the black man is intended to give him the power to work out deals with the major political parties, and when these are not possible, to lend his support to the independent parties or reform groups which, in a democracy, are constantly emerging and reemerging.

There is plenty of scope for such alliances today and considerable evidence of success where they have been tried. The education of black children, for example, has recently become the very active concern of many white as well as black educators and sociologists. There is no good reason why this interest can not be extended to rural education in the South or to the reinstitution of compulsory education in Mississippi. It was repealed there in 1956 despite the statistics which showed that Mississippi had the highest illiteracy rate in the country.

Or low-cost interest rates on mortgages—this was once the privilege of middle-income home owners and returning war veterans only. Recent legislation in response to civil rights demands, as well as pressure from poor families, both black and white, extended the policy to low-cost housing.

Or the billions of dollars spent on highway construction and on subsidizing commuter transportation, both designed to facilitate the move to the suburbs —black and white city dwellers can present a united front for similar support of urban roads and transportation systems.

Or the seven per cent Federal tax incentive for capital investment, used largely for industrial building in the suburbs—a slightly larger allowance for ghetto or fringe ghetto investment might steer the building in that direction. But pressure is needed to affect that percentage.

Pressure is necessary to push state governments into appropriating the very modest sum required for the distribution of surplus foods which the Federal government supplies. Or to force states to put up matching funds which will entitle them to Federal money for aid to families with dependent children—twenty-one states, not all in the South, are today foregoing more than one hundred million dollars in Federal money annually to avoid providing help of their own. Surely black and white poor and not so poor white liberals and black leaders who have known the feel of poverty can make common cause out of this problem. And the new welfare plan may mean change here.

And blacks who believe that the problems of the central cities are more urgent than continued hostilities in Vietnam or anywhere else they might break out have the responsibility not only of making their opinions heard but of joining the white voices that are clamoring for settlement and a change in foreign policy. Whether they are right or wrong does not alter the fact that disagreement is part of the democratic process. The result is usually compromise, with some victory gained by each side. But compromise is the principle on which the American government is structured. It has so far proven more satisfactory to most people than the totalitarian societies built around absolutes.

The black thrust today is for organizing its bloc into a third party. Some say that the initial impulse for this idea came out of the challenge of the Mississipppi Freedom Democratic Party at the 1964 Democratic national convention. Blacks brought evidence then to show that the regular Mississippi Democratic delegation was racist and demanded to be seated as the representatives of the blacks in Mississippi. They were not successful in 1964. But in 1968, the Democratic party announced in advance of the convention that a black delegation from Mississippi would have legal representation there. And a compromise at the convention seated the all–white delegation from Georgia and a new integrated representation, each to have equal voting strength.

The Mississippi Freedom Democratic Party is not actually and was never intended to be a national third party. It simply sought, as an organized body within the state Democratic party, to secure representation for the black man. The goal that the Black Panthers seem to be working out in a formal merger with S.N.C.C. is for a separate party for the black man. A name, the Peace and Freedom Party, was chosen and in July 1968, the candidates that the party hoped to get on the November 1968 ballot were selected.

Candidate for President was Eldridge Cleaver, Minister of Information of the Black Panther party. Cleaver polled 195,134 votes; Dick Gregory, running on both the Peace and Freedom Party and what he calls his New Party, polled 148,622. More black votes went to Hubert Humphrey in the hope that they would help to defeat both Wallace and Nixon. Most black people in the United States are realists.

Some parts of the Black Panthers' political program would probably be acceptable to the white liberal. Black Panthers have expressed their opposition to rioting and have been willing to work in close cooperation—but on an equal basis—with white groups. They want to police their own ghettos with blacks who live in the community. And they believe that blacks have the right to self-determination.

Other Black Panther demands strike out at American institutions in a way which even white liberals find difficult to take. Black Panthers urge the release of all black prisoners from jails, a legal system requiring a black jury in legal action where a black is involved, and a choice for black people, as well as for other minorities, to govern themselves as "separate nations" or to "integrate into Babylon." They also demand reparations for past cheap labor and a transfer to the community of the means of production when a white businessman fails to provide full employment.

No one quite knows the numerical strength of the Black Panthers throughout the country although the press has made much of their supposed armed strength which, they claim, is to be used only to defend themselves against the "brutalization of the occupying army," that is, the police. They are beginning to organize in Los Angeles, Philadelphia, Newark, New York, and other cities. Their refusal to divulge the size of their membership has been variously attributed to hesitation about revealing how small it is or to strategy about hiding its potential force. And, in 1969 they began to speak in Marxist-Leninist phraseology which calls for revolt by black and white.

A Negro political party is not likely to get its candidate elected to the Presidency in the immediate future. Even impassioned Black Panther and S.N.C.C. leaders concede that. But it can siphon off enough votes to put some key states in doubt in a tight election. The Democratic party evidently gave this possibility some thought. The decision to seat the black delegation from Mississippi and the two delegations from Georgia at the 1968 national convention may well have been the result of such consideration. The victory must, in any case, be interpreted as an example of the power of black political pressure, supported by the Northern Democratic white liberals on the Credentials Committee—probably for both idealistic and strategic reasons. Whether this power will continue to be exerted as a bloc or as a separate political party will in part depend on the course of the two major parties. According to the 1967 figures in the *Congressional Quarterly*, the Dixiecrat-Republican coalition won thirty-seven out of the fifty times it decided to vote together on Congressional legislation. They are, in effect, forming a third party of their own. If such actions continue, black in-party blocs may have a significant—and perhaps welcome— role to play in revitalizing the liberal Republican and Democratic forces that have not allied themselves with the coalition. The placement of a black candidate, the Reverend Channing Philips, in nomination for the presidency by a white man at the Democratic Convention, may be an indication of Democratic Party intent to attract the black vote on a natinoal level.

Evangelists of the separate black state, are, of course, against any such mergers. For them, a gesture of white agreement is countersubversion, an attempt to split black unity or to buy off black opposition to white policies. Most black people feel that their revolution has passed this critical stage. Blacks are too aware by now of buying-off techniques. They see too clearly their own role as decision and change-makers. And they intend to employ their unity to achieve what they want through the leverage of the democratic system. Some blacks have become so intent about political solidarity that they are afraid even to move out of the ghetto lest this diffuse their voting strength. They have to be reminded that residence does not affect state and national elections and that a black bloc can be maintained in an integrated America, too.

It may be that black separatists are screaming for blood as well as for power. The inhuman repression to which the black man in America has been subjected can indeed generate such desires. For their part, black moderate militants prefer construction to vengeful assault. They may not love white America either. But they are reconceiving it as a white-black America. The growing awareness on the part of the black man, the climate of black social pressure, and the steadily changing political scene may all be steps in this direction.

13.
THE NEGRO
AND THE
GREAT SOCIETY

The hopes of former President Johnson's Great Society program have, in some respects, far exceeded expectations. Progress in implementing Title II, Part A of the 1964 Economic Opportunity Act in the large urban ghettos where the program is functioning has been so good, it seems to have begun to frighten even the establishment that dreamed up the idea. This section of the law authorizes Federal financial assistance for community action programs, developed and conducted at a community level, to combat poverty. It is based on the belief that local residents know their own community better than most outsiders and that they can be expected to "commit their ideas and resources" and to assume both leadership and responsibility for developing and carrying out local–action programs. The concept of community involvement is spelled out in the definition which states that a community action program must be developed,

conducted, and administered with the maximum fea-
sible participation of the residents of the area. The
role of the Federal government is limited to providing financial assistance for the cost of such programs and, when requested, counsel and help in
developing them.

Appropriations for community action programs
come out of "versatile funds" which are not ear-
marked for specifically designated projects. The local
poor thus have the opportunity to work out the kinds
of programs that they see as best meeting their own
needs. Blacks have demonstrated an unanticipated
sharpness in analyzing these needs. Most of their programs are designed to develop among the poor an
awareness both of their rights and of the channels
through which they can make their demands. This
foray into self–help has, of course, not gone un-
noticed.

A vigilant Congress has responded to the challenge.
In December 1967, it amended the Economic Opportunity Act with a law prohibiting the use of community action funds for political purposes. Voter
registration is apparently considered a political purpose since community action money, in accordance
with the new law, can no longer be spent to get a
community's citizens registered at the polls. Lobbying
for more community action money is proscribed, too.
The Hatch Act, passed in 1966, stated that community
action funds could definitely not be used in this way.

The 1968 legislature also threatened to dismantle
the Economic Opportunity Act structure. It is true
that this action was taken in a climate of public reaction to mismanagement and to theft of poverty

funds. Blacks, who see their own misdeeds as in-
finitesimal when compared with the white man's,
accused Congress of using the scandals as a smoke-
screen for their own purposes. A bill was proposed
to remove the ear-marked sections of the program—
Title I, A, B, and C: Youth Programs; Title II, B:
Basic Adult Education; Title III: Special Programs
to Combat Poverty in Rural Areas; Title IV: Employment and Investment Incentives; and Title V: Work
Experience Program—from the Office of Economic
Opportunity, the Federal body now administering
the anti-poverty effort. They were to be parcelled out,
instead, to variously related agencies, the Job Corps
(Title I), for example, to the Department of Labor,
and Head Start (Title II, B), to Health, Education,
and Welfare, two moves which the newly elected President Nixon put into effect through executive order.
The idea was to make an even more piecemeal plan
out of a centrally organized anti-poverty thrust. The
Congress gave way on this measure—but at a price.
One-third of the Board of Directors of every central
community action program must now be composed of
government officials.

As currently organized, the Board of Directors,
called by varying names in different cities, towns,
rural areas, and Indian reservations where the community action program has been introduced, consists
of a maximum of fifty-one members. In New York
City, where it is known as the Council Against Poverty, twenty-five of the members are delegates of the
poor, seventeen or exactly one-third are government
officials, and nine represent city-wide agencies cooperating in the anti-poverty effort. The Economic

Opportunity Act stipulates that public or non-profit private agencies or "a combination thereof" may be used to conduct, administer, or coordinate anti-poverty programs. It makes provision for financial assistance to be granted to these agencies when they aid in the development and operation of action programs "which are of sufficient size and scope to show promise of concrete progress toward the elimination of poverty and a cause or causes of poverty."

Settlement houses, churches, citizens' associations, professional organizations, public and private school systems, and other similar interested community groups have all been involved in developing some of the less controversial aspects of Title II of the Economic Opportunity Act. The Head Start program is a particular favorite. Who can argue with the values of providing enriching experiences for pre-school age children to help them overcome the handicaps of limited environmental opportunities during their most formative years?

Community action ideas which conservatively oriented institutions do not want—or do not dare—to explore are being taken on by local residents who form themselves into an agency for just such a purpose. Programs in consumer education, in tenant organization, in welfare rights action—as well as the now outlawed voter registration drives—are all examples of action efforts that ghetto groups have with the aid of Federal funds begun on their own.

The distribution of Federal anti-poverty funds differs slightly from community to community. In New York City—the paradigm for a number of large ghetto areas which hope to follow its lead and the example to many white governors and mayors of the kind of program that must, at all costs, be kept out of their areas—the Council Against Poverty has designated twenty-five sections of the city as poverty areas. Each area is administered by a local community corporation with at least one-third representation of the poor on its board of directors, which controls the local anti-poverty money. A group applying for a grant must first submit a proposal, stating exactly how the money is to be used and outlining the step-by-step procedure, including the use of personnel, through which the program is to be implemented. When a proposal is approved by the Council Against Poverty, the new delegated agency may begin to hire the professional, community, and technical assistants who will, as indicated in the proposal, administer and develop the program. The approved grant includes authorized money for the payment of their salaries.

When help is needed—and it frequently is by local resident groups—in organizing the proposal or in writing the specialized language usually expected in a grant application, an operational staff provides it. New York City's operational staff, attached to the Council Against Poverty, is called the Community Development Agency. The aid it offers extends beyond the formulation of the request for funds. The Community Development Agency also assists in coordinating the various facets of an approved program and in finding needed key personnel. When a program gets started, the Community Development Agency has the responsibility of supervising and evaluating it.

But the Council Against Poverty has reserved for itself the right to decide on program priorities. It may, for example, believe that consumer education is far more important than any of the requests made by local community groups; it can, if it so deems, then apportion a percentage of the area allocation for a suitable program in consumer education. Or it may consider that the supplementary health service program for which funds are requested by one local group is only half as urgent as the education action program that another group is envisioning and allocate its money accordingly. Or it may, in assigning funds for city-wide community action programs, give more money for the Urban League's Operation Open City plan than to the ASPIRA project which seeks out promising young Puerto Rican students and helps them to get into college. The power of a central community action board is indeed great. The in-fighting between Negroes and Puerto Ricans for positions on the local board and for their respective portions of available funds is frequent. And the desire of government officials to share some of this money-dispensing power, if only in the interests of self-protection against an unexpected manifestation of black strength is, of course, understandable.

Most probably, no one quite anticipated, back in the days when the Economic Opportunity Act was being discussed and assembled, that its community action programs would become the means by which one black community after another militantly sought to affect social change. But then practically nobody in those days particularly equated the Negro with poverty or made a special effort to identify the reasons for his condition. The tendency seems to have been to lump all unemployed and underemployed together and to try to think of some encompassing solution for the problems of *the poor.*

Certainly, few sociologists bothered to pinpoint why some poor were poorer than others or stayed poor longer or abounded in matriarchal family structures or were inclined as a group to be uninterested in the politics of a larger society, to lag in the development of protest or self-help associations of their own, and to participate in these, when they were somehow—and very occasionally—organized, on a passive level, if at all. Sociologists, looking for answers in 1964 as a first step, might have separated the poor among the Negroes, the Puerto Ricans, the Mexican-Americans, and the American Indians from the poor of other North American ethnic groups. They would probably have observed, too, that the poor in the separated group were, on the whole, more withdrawn, apathetic, and hopeless.

Those sociologists who were aware, even in 1964, of this mood of "anomie" and those who spoke of a culture or subculture of poverty which financial security does not quickly or easily change, might well have recommended the community action programs as a beginning in treating the causation of Negro poverty. Nobody seems to have asked for their opinion, however. And nobody, least of all a Congress intent on carrying forward the frontier spirit of the Kennedy administration, seems to have given much thought to the underlying philosophy of the programs: some poverty problems require changes in the social structure; change can be deliberately induced by group action.

Just what the Congress expected from a law that gave the poor the opportunity to become less poor through their own ideas and leadership can only be surmised. What it got was a direct attack on black inertia. Nothing better could have been designed to give the Negro his motivation for involvement. If he was running the show, he didn't have to feel hopeless any more. He could induce change.

And to the consternation of that and of successive Congresses, the black man, in his community action programs, is doing exactly that. He has developed, too, a pride about what he is accomplishing, a feeling of belonging and counting that may, better than some employment training programs, qualify him to compete on more equal terms in today's society.

Most community action programs are intended to provide better services to a poverty area which, in cities, is largely black, even if the Eighty-eighth Congress did not quite realize this. But the black man knows it and plans accordingly. A community legal services program, for example, starts out with the premise that the average ghetto black for one reason or another does not always get justice in the courts. The program therefore provides him with legal counsel—which, incidentally, has won case after case for blacks in the last few years—with legal representation at police stations, legal assistance in making investigations when these are needed, and legal advice about contracts, leases, and tenants' rights. A recently funded program works to assure the continuing availability of empathetic legal counsel. Volunteers with a knowledge of ghetto problems or a ghetto background have been enrolled in law schools for this purpose.

The consciousness of actual ghetto needs guides all other community action endeavors. A community action housing program assumes that the white establishment is not really overconcerned about ghetto housing conditions. The first item on its agenda is then to make a block-by-block survey of building violations. The information it gathers is subsequently used as documentary evidence in formal complaints and requests.

A community action education program proceeds with the knowledge that a white school system and black ghetto parents have little understanding of each other. Members thus involve themselves in school-community relations, in decentralization plans, and on Operation Head Start, in making sure that blacks serve on the parent advisory committees.

A community social service referral program compiles lists of neighborhood services to which blacks are entitled with full information about names, addresses, hours of accessibility, etc. A welfare rights action program apprises black welfare applicants and recipients of their rights and also tries to raise the level of their discontent in relation to subsistence welfare standards. A community health program involves blacks in planning where ghetto hospitals should be built and how health services can be organized to meet ghetto problems most realistically.

Thousands of community action programs have been started in the cities and towns of the nation. Always, the goal seems to be to goad the structure into accommodating the special needs of the blacks. This is quite a switch from the behavior of the "other" poor, who have tried to fit themselves into the patterns of the structure. Perhaps this latter effort is what the Congress was hoping for when it passed the Economic Opportunity Act, with Title II, A section included.

But the Congress apparently did not make the distinction that blacks never seem to forget. The white poor live with the prospect of one day becoming part of the power structure. Its prejudices and indifference have little to do with them. For ghetto blacks, such attitudes are synonymous with the white structure. Black community action groups see as their first aim the removal of the effects of racial discrimination both on ghetto services and ghetto apathy. The enforcement of a building code on a Harlem street then assumes a significance beyond the intent of the action. Success represents new power and has meaningful implications for the future.

Change is almost always a threat. It is particularly upsetting to a predominantly white society so thoroughly conditioned to black humility. The 25 per cent reduction in the 1967-68 anti-poverty appropriations and the cut in 1968 summer job funds from a projected seventy-five million dollars to thirteen million may be interpreted as the expediencies of a guns or butter choice. But some have called it retaliation and point to the removal in December 1967 of a number of community action programs from the versatile funds area to Economic Opportunity Act titles where they can be more tightly controlled. The transfer involves no fiscal advantage, whatsoever. It may, how-

ever, symbolize the new foresight of a now cautious
Congress.

Official policy seems to be writing off most of the
Economic Opportunity Act as a failure. Reduced
appropriations may be continued for Head Start,
Health Services, Legal Services, the Youth Corps,
and the Job Corps, but probably not for the nitty
gritty action program. States that never permitted
these programs to function within their borders are
already beginning to feel less threatened by social
disapproval.

The new emphasis is on employment. Ghetto blacks
have no objections. They merely hope that the job-
creating opportunities under consideration do not
follow the pattern of the Manpower Development and
Training Act where a good deal of the training has
been for such work as packaging, food distribution,
and routine office practices. Most blacks say that they
have had enough of these dead-end jobs. If they are
going to be trained, they want it to be for employment that has upgrading potential.

They are not at all sure, however, that the new
concern about jobs is the basic reason for the change
they see in the offing. They are more inclined to suspect that the difficulties which whites experience in
fully accepting blacks as equals—and some blacks
are charitable enough to admit that this may occasionally be unconscious—contribute more significantly
to the new thinking. White liberals may not contest
the rights of blacks to better services. But even they
shudder at the language in which demands are frequently couched, and condemn or deplore the black

aggressive attitude. They, too, have been known to say that blacks have gone too far.

The point that black leaders make at this time is that whites are unwilling or unable—to the accusers it makes little difference—to concede to blacks the human frailties that they accept in themselves. If they did, they would more readily understand that people who have never been listened to before are prone to indulge in the release of taunts and threats. At this stage in the black-white dialogue, they are not completely sure that the establishment will hear anything else.

It is this refusal to accord to blacks the equal privilege of error that their leaders are now calling attention to as the new and most ironic twist in discriminatory attitudes. They attribute to it much of the criticism that has been leveled at poorly planned or mismanaged community action programs. They protest that if they have sometimes planned poorly, it is because they are unable, as anyone might be, to cope with the constant uncertainties of budget allocations. Congressional appropriations for the fiscal year July 1967 to July 1968 were not finalized until December 1967. And if there has been some mismanagement, they add, it is because the white man has no monopoly on dishonesty.

One error which those involved in community action programs make note of on their own is the tendency by black leaders to become protective about their own particular programs, so much so that they sometimes forget to see them as only a part of a larger entity. But this disadvantage is outweighed by the opportunity that funding provides for leadership training. Hopelessness discouraged most emerging black leadership before. Those few who persisted in trying to achieve something for and with their communities had to do so after working hours. Funding now enables them to give full time to their efforts.

Funding provides jobs, too, for thousands of black professionals and clerical and manual workers involved in implementing various facets of the Economic Opportunity Act. The ghetto wonders what will happen to these people if the program is dissolved. Other federally financed projects may be started. But surely, the ghetto says, no project can be as important as helping a depressed community to get on its feet. Even comparatively unskilled black workers, employed in community action programs as cleaners or delivery men have felt motivated here. This has been their program and they were contributing in their way to its progress.

No great effort is presumably being made to organize any federally financed work program. The drive is rather in the direction of involving private industry in hiring more black workers, particularly among the hard-core urban unemployed. Unfortunately, no spectacular success can be anticipated from this move. A 1967 Bureau of Labor Statistics study estimated that it would take more than six hundred thousand new jobs to reduce the unemployment rate in poverty areas to the same level as in non-poverty areas. The results of federally subsidized training programs for the unemployed hard-core have so far been far from encouraging. New York State made 6,900 out of a hoped for 40,000 job placements in 1967. Chicago found that only 28 per cent of the nearly 1,500 graduates of its Jobs Now project held onto the jobs that were found for them. Salaries were fairly good, some over $6,000 per year. But that was, in most cases, not enough to get a family out of the ghetto. And the jobs did not have, as they do in community action programs, a feeling of identification which carries with it the hope of destroying the ghetto forever.

Black ghetto leaders do not see the community action section of the Economic Opportunity Act as a panacea. They know that it can not solve the complexity of social, economic, and racial problems that black poverty means. But, on the other hand, blacks maintain, neither can a job, per se. Full Negro employment during World War II did not do much to help the black man move either physically or spiritually out of his ghetto. Community action programs by affording him participation and leadership in planning for his own welfare have at least begun the process of deghettoization. Many factors may make it impossible for the ghetto black to move quickly out of his neighborhood. His newly acquired sophistication about the democratic process, however, has already reduced some of the ills that define his neighborhood as a ghetto.

Nor do black leaders view the polarized systems that the programs often set up—an education action program versus a Board of Education, for example, or a welfare action program versus a city Department of Welfare—as a permanent or even temporarily desirable way of life. What they are looking forward to is a hooking in of the ideas they have developed with existing systems. Some of their auxiliary services have already been incorporated into city services. Paraprofessionals throughout the country are working in schools, hospitals, clinics, welfare offices, community education projects and other community oriented areas to provide communication between program and ghetto resident.

But even more important, in the opinion of black leaders, than these opportunities for mutual understanding and meaningful employment, is the need for the ghetto to continue its work of making the establishment responsive to all of its needs. Whether the community action programs do or do not survive, the black man intends to use the know–how he has acquired to make the structure accountable to him. He has a firmer awareness of his rights and an understanding of the role of government officials as public servants. He would prefer a negotiating relationship where he can present his point of view peaceably. But he has no strong hesitations about bucking City Hall. He has decided, as the revolutionary Fanon exhorted, that he will no longer be the slave of the slavery which once destroyed his ancestors.

14.
WHO
AM I?

These are the days when the black man is watchful, suspicious, and always ready to burst out with his protests. Basically, they advise the white man not to try to capture him, by which he means to make him into a white Negro, and not to imagine for one moment that a white man can any longer tell him what to do because, "I'm my own man now. Hear? My own man!"

The American Negro's search for identity has so far given him one homeland in the distant past and one in the still unforeseeable future. The homeland in the past is, of course, Africa to which he has deliberately attached himself, partly out of an identification with the men of dark skin there, but mainly because his forefathers once lived there. The customs of his tribal ancestors have not survived the years, either as a culture or religion, making the identity rather doubtful here. But the American Negro's obvious need is for a feeling of belonging and evidently Africa gives him more of that than present day America.

It is the same need that prompts the cries for a separate state, in or outside of the United States, any place actually that the black man may consider his own. Even some strong anti-separatist blacks are lately expressing their support for a black state. "We don't all of us have to go into it," they say. "We just have to know that it's there in case we ever do want to go. It's no different from the Jews wanting a state of their own." The loneliness of the black man in America is apparently deeper and more painful than most Americans can ever wholly realize.

To bolster his sense of personal identity, the black man has launched his program of self-assertion. He is defining himself in terms of the social status he has gained through the civil rights struggle and by the criteria of economic sufficiency and political autonomy that essentially constitute his black power campaign. He is reaching out, as he does in his search for a homeland, for the external strengths that a white man usually takes for granted. At the moment, they are still tenuous supports. Neither the current stance of militancy nor the new pride of black purpose has yet eradicated the feelings of self-doubt and inferiority that are evidently the Negro's heritage in America. He probably still has a long way to go before he knows a sustaining sense of security as a man.

In the white community, manhood is usually equated with responsibility. This may vary with age and social level. But responsibility almost always means preparing oneself to make a living, giving up years for education in order to make a better and more satisfying living, providing for a wife and children, planning for the future of children, and, in some cases, becoming involved in community obligations which affect the well-being of one's family, neighborhood, and country. Persistence, sacrifice, delayed gratifications are all accepted as norms in the behavior of a man.

In the ghetto, manhood is extremely important. The white man may, and usually does, call the American Negro "boy." But the word *man* is undoubtedly one of the most popular in-appelations among the Negroes themselves. Black male children address each other as "man" almost from the time they are able to talk.

The white standards of manhood—and they are the values of the Negro middle class, as well—have little practical meaning for the average ghetto black. He lives with the day-to-day problems which rarely afford him the time or the peace to think about the future. They are the lot of the poor and the diffident who seem to struggle principally to keep from getting poorer. The middle-class white usually has to have such problems spelled out for him one by one for he can not easily anticipate them—or even always believe them. For example: a black man does not come to evening school to improve his literacy skills because his boss frowns—and this can have all kinds of implications—when he watches the clock so as to leave exactly on time; a black woman does not keep her morning appointment with the school guidance counsellor or report to her afternoon job as a domestic because "Housing" has advised her to wait for the exterminator and there is no superintendent to open the door for him and he still hasn't shown up and both the guidance counselor and her employer are getting tired of this "undependability." A young black mother deprives her child of a Head Start opportunity because the interviewer in the program wants to know where she lives and how long she's been living there and, until she gets a job—which she cannot do before she finds some school for her child for a few hours a day, at least—she is staying with relatives in a project and, if this is discovered, they will lose the apartment. Separately, the problems seem insignificant, ridiculous even to those who prefer to criticize. Together, they tend to put off serious considerations of ambitions that require effort and concentration and single-mindedness.

At best, the average ghetto black has not been inclined to believe that his sacrifices will achieve for him the goals that whites can usually count on. Through the years, he has developed alternative satisfactions that have seemed to him more relevant to life in the ghetto. Physical prowess has been one of his chief definitions of manhood. The prizefighter, the young black who is quick with his fists, the black who is ready to take on all comers and then, movie-like, to strut coolly off, is a hero in the ghetto. A Don Juan relationship with women is another ghetto criterion for manhood. The black who makes it with the ladies, who has them catering to his every whim is, in the admiring eyes of other ghetto blacks, really a man. Challenging authority is still another measure of manhood. Gambling, playing the numbers, standing up to the police are all, in part, acts of defiance which help blacks feel more triumphantly manly. The recent challenges of violent confrontation, particularly by young blacks, are, to an extent, also motivated by the drive to prove black manliness.

But until recently, it was still the white man who was referred to as *the man* in the ghetto. Bravado did not really convince the ghetto black that he was actually very much of a man. How could it when he had to go out into the white society with his feet shuffling? When he had to come back and again tell his wife that he could not get a job? When he had to explain to the children who looked up to him as all powerful that he could do nothing about changing the law—or the custom—which excluded them from a white playground? When he could not even shout from the housetops that black children were as good as white children? When he was not even sure that he believed it himself?

Things have begun to change, however. Black pressure has modified white attitudes, expectations, and practices. The ghetto black is thinking of himself as more of a man, and concomitantly, accepting some of the non-ghetto standards for manhood as applicable to him.

Perhaps the most important change for the black man involves the hope that for him, too, there is a future. When he can look forward to better possibilities, he is able to accept the disciplines of effort and planning. Concepts of building and developing are now replacing the ghetto goals of immediate satisfaction. The great concern is with the young people for whom college and professions and a meaningful place in society are no longer wishful dreams. Black parents are intent on seeing to it that their children get the best possible education. The issues in the controversy between Ocean Hill-Brownsville and the striking teachers and supervisors may have involved such highly controversial questions as political control of the school system by the mayor, the fate of the merit system, the right of local school boards to community control, the rights of teachers in a decentralization plan, the harassment of strikers, and the accusation by the Ocean Hill-Brownsville administration of sabotage of its experiment by strikers. But the chief worry of the great majority of black parents was about the school time that black children lose when teachers strike. Black children can not afford to lose school time. They have too much catching up to do in a white world.

The talents and abilities of the young—rather than the objects or possessions that used to constitute the status symbols—are now considered the resources of the future. Ghetto blacks depend on them for a continuation of their revolution. They have no illusions that this is anywhere near over, though most of them believe it will eventually move from the streets into the councils of power. They don't intend that it be over until the white man relinquishes his position in the master-slave relationship. Their rejection of white help grows out of the conviction that this is the white man's way—even when he does not completely recognize it—of perpetuating his master role. They trust only themselves to do "what is good for the black man."

The new young are being brought up with a strong feeling of responsibility to this phase of the black revolution. They are expected to take their place on those councils of power, to exert their influence in the interests of the black community. On the level of commitment to what is good for blacks, the unity of black people is daily becoming firmer. The black middle class, for so long isolated from ghetto needs and motivated now, perhaps, only by the common experience of racial insult and exclusion, speaks out these days about its involvement.

Ideas about what is good for blacks include concerned political representation. This automatically eliminates the white man who may, from time to time, have felt sorry about the ghetto but never particularly empathized with its problems. As one more example of what they mean, blacks point to the white man's concern about narcotics addiction now that his own children have been going to pot parties and getting hooked on heroin and using L.S.D. When black children were taking drugs—and they have been doing it for years, even buying it in the schools; official United States Bureau of Narcotics figures indicate that addiction is heavily concentrated in low-income Negro neighborhoods—he checked it off as a statistic. Sometimes, he also called it a racial characteristic.

And ghetto blacks insist, as always, that the black man must be in charge of the delivery of services to his own community. This is again an expression of black need for concerned administration and of the distrust of white feelings of responsiveness either to ghetto realities or to the black man's right to make the decisions that affect his own welfare.

The slant that is new in the definition of what is good for the black man is the increasing concentration on the connections that can open the doors to middle-class opportunities. This may come as a shock in a revolution which has been so defensive about the life style of its poor. As recently as 1966, Floyd McKissick, the then CORE director, stated, "My major criticism of the report (the Moynihan report about the Negro family) is that it assumes that middle-class American values are the correct ones for everyone in America. Just because Moynihan believes in the middle-class values doesn't mean that they are the best for everyone in America. Moynihan thinks everyone should have a family structure like his own."

McKissick's theme has been reiterated at thousands of rallies and workshops and discussion sessions since. But change in the direction of middle-class goals seems to be part of the process of all revolutions of the poor. What is surprising in the black revolution is only that the change came so rapidly.

The ghetto black is emerging as an aspiring man, and not in terms of the crutch he used in the ghetto when every sentence ended with man—"Want to know something, man?"—to assure himself that he was one. He is emerging as a family man, with a new sense of responsibility to his wife, his children, his family structure. Most of his concentration on contacts is related to his concern for his children. He wants to learn just what to do to prepare his bright young son who is interested in chemistry for a career in science, where to buy the books and the magazines (which he can often borrow from a library, if only he knew about the service), that the boy wants to read, how to enroll his small daughter in the Saturday morning art classes that he has heard some museum provides, and, for his middle daughter, which junior high school has a good reputation "for making the kids work." They are minimal enough ambitions, from the white man's point of view. For the blacks, they represent an identification with mainstream values and aspirations that, in the case of the large majority, are totally new. Only a ghetto-born white man—coming out of what was once the white ghetto, that is—can begin to understand why connections are so important for poor blacks and how their lack can deprive a child forever of the opportunity to live up to his potential.

Both family responsibility and pride are novel emotions for many ghetto black males. The recurrent pattern over the years has been one of family breakdown with the father out of the house and the working mother caring for children who wandered the streets during her absence and learned much more about dope sellers, numbers runners, prostitution, casual sexual affairs, and crimes to beat the system than they did about chemistry or art. The proportion of non-white families with only a female head was 23.7 per cent in 1966 as contrasted with 8.9 per cent among whites. Illegitimate birth rates among non-whites today exceed 50 per cent in the ghettos of many large cities. Rates of juvenile delinquency, venereal disease, financial dependence upon Aid to Families of Dependent Children, or upon general public assistance are all much higher in disadvantaged areas than in other parts of large cities. And not surprisingly, the proportion of children from ages six through nineteen who attend school is considerably lower in homes where one or no parent is present than in homes with both parents there to make up a family unit.

A close correlation also seems to exist between the

number of non-white married women separated from their husbands each year and the unemployment rate among non-white males twenty years old and over. In 1967, the proportion of married men either divorced or separated from their wives was more than twice as high among unemployed non-white men as among employed non-white men. The figures only sum up an old and familiar cycle: a man cannot get a stable job at an adequate wage; he can not provide for his family; he loses status and respect in his own mind and in the mind of his family; the struggle of continuing family responsibility becomes unbearable; desertion is one way out, probably the most practical way, for the family is likely to receive welfare aid much more easily when the supposed wage earner is not in the home.

Poverty usually exacts a high toll. When the poverty grows basically out of discrimination and in its turn breeds feelings of male hopelessness, certain patterns seem almost inevitable. One of these among blacks is the tendency for women to dominate the life of the family. The high rate of out-of-wedlock births is one reason for this matriarchal structure. Another is the evident ability of the Negro woman to fare better personally and economically in the outside white world than her husband. As the chief breadwinner, she becomes the actual head of the home. Her dominance frequently extends to her husband, who, if he is still living in the home, may not be there long. He may try drugs first to help him blot out what is happening to him. Or he may subject his wife and children to a few drunken brawls as the only means left to him of expressing his authority. Either way, he has begun to separate himself from his family. His departure simply completes his alienation—usually for good—from the stabilities of a family life.

Blacks have a lot to say about why more Negro women manage to earn some sort of living in the outside white world than Negro men. They maintain that whites prefer to hire Negro women because women are less competitive and therefore less threatening to the white man. A black man expects both a peer relationship—as a man—with his employer and co-workers and an opportunity to get ahead on a job. The denial of both of these conditions is interpreted by blacks as a deliberate intent to destroy the male black ego which they liken to castration. One of the goals of the black revolution is to get rid of the effects of this conditioning by establishing the black man in a peer relationship with the white man.

Almost all black leaders are male today. The only exception is Congresswoman Shirley Chisholm. This is official black policy. It is planned to develop the black man's capacity to discuss, negotiate, wheel and deal, and eventually, to compete as a man in a male competitive world. The concept has elicited a positive response from black women who seem to understand exactly why it is important and are content to let their men become their spokesmen. It is increasingly the black male now who deals with the landlord, the schools, and the various other city departments in which the family may be involved. It is only the black male who now works out the strategy of the black revolution.

As a social movement, the black revolution has lived through a number of phases and evolved varying philosophies and tactics. The civil rights protests that followed the 1954 Supreme Court decision and culminated in the 1964 Civil Rights Act are probably illustrative of its initial design. The Act may have laid to rest all vestiges of legal discrimination. But the decade of civil rights protest was evidently also the period when de facto segregation moved rapidly in to take over where legal segregation left off. Bayard Rustin summarized the distinction when he said in 1963 that the civil rights movement was "now concerned not merely with removing the barriers to full equality but with achieving the fact of equality." The black power revolution that started in 1966 enlisted all blacks in the battle for "the fact of equality," some to loot and to burn, others to appraise the conflict more soberly and to work through the democratic process for the power that could make equality a fact. At this point, the black revolution seems to be in the process of evaluating itself. Recent policy decisions point to a willingness on the part of black leaders to work with the whites—if the relationship is on a peer basis. The militant Black Panthers have decided to operate within the establishment as a political party. S.N.C.C., involved with the Black Panthers in organizing this party, has politely worked out a divorce from Stokely Carmichael evidently because of his separatist attitudes. And in the interests of more enduring black power, the current emphasis of the black revolution appears to be breaking what James Baldwin describes as a self-perpetuating system that leads blacks —who are denied responsibility—to cultivate the values of irresponsibility and to talk a code language of jargon and obscenity, the key to which is hatred.

It is still a black ghetto revolution. Its fundamental premise has simply been extended from the concept that only blacks are concerned enough to fight their revolution to the thought that only when the blacks themselves utilize the full range of their personal resources to cope with their situation can any meaningful solution be achieved. At this stage in American history, the Negro is not yet accepted by his fellow citizens as a fellow man. But his struggle to define himself has so far given him enough assurance to proclaim to his countrymen, "I am a black man" and to go on with his revolution on that basis.

15.
WHAT
DO "THEY"
THINK?

What they—meaning the white people—think may be of little importance to the militant black caught up in the triumph of his assertive and retributive moment. Unfortunately, this is not also his moment of truth. The reactions of whites to the tactics and progress of the black revolution can not realistically be separated from its eventual outcome.

Liberal white forces at this point seem somewhat disoriented in their stand on the black revolution. The issues were clearer when mass civil disobedience served to protest local laws or practices that violated rights guaranteed by the Constitution. Most liberal whites could at least define their positions as morally unambiguous when the marches and the boycotts and the sit-ins struck out against the traditional citadels of legal discrimination in the South.

But both the locale of the battle and the lines of the attack have changed. War is being waged in the ghetto streets of the North. The protagonists are now the ghetto rebels, restive, violent, ready to condemn American society as racist or sick, versus a white power structure, rigid, entrenched, and quick to reply, with soothing self-righteousness, that the ghetto revolution is characterized not by its expressed ideals of equality and justice but by thievery, the thwarting of all authority, and by considerable anti-semitism, to boot. The statement by Lawrence Lundry, black radical leader from Chicago, in which he said that the White House Conference of November 1965 was dominated by "whites and Jews" has become historic. It is often quoted by Jewish white liberals who see the Negro push into the professions and the Civil Service jobs as a deliberate attempt at replacement. Jews can be both as practical and as paranoiac as blacks in interpreting attitudes and tendencies.

When liberal whites, the long-time friends of the Negro and still able sometimes to separate the black tactics of desperation from the black goals of freedom, are joined by conservatives and downright reactionaries, retaliation is sure to follow. Feelings range now from more than mild disapproval to an antipathy which has proven itself revengeful. The response to urban guerrilla warfare has been a definite turn to the political Right. State legislatures have passed or are in the process of passing "Shoot to Kill" and "No Knock" bills, the latter endorsing house entries without a search warrant. The United States Congress disapproved the original anti-rat bill (which required an appropriation too small to threaten the support of the Vietnam war even for a day) then passed it under protest, after considerably trimming down the projected appropriation, and has only recently voted the reduced amount into existence. Congressional decisions have also cut the Model Cities program in half and taken steps to emasculate the anti-poverty thrust of the Economic Opportunity Act. The Open Housing Bill could not even get to the floor of Congress before Martin Luther King's death. Its passage later is generally regarded as a testimonial to a black man who was non-violent.

On the local level, the response has run the gamut from fighting back to complete withdrawal. SPONGE, the organization in Brooklyn designed as a Society to Prevent Only Negroes from Getting Everything, is typical of small group resentment throughout the country. The black man is castigated for having lowered Civil Service standards—a high school diploma is no longer needed—for having debased teaching requirements—in New York City, fewer educational credits are expected—and for having practically destroyed the meaning of professionalism. The paraprofessional, it is feared in many circles, will soon be taking over; and, of course, the elegibility requirements for college entrance have been lowered in order to admit the Negro. The Negro is accused, in short of trying to get everything for nothing, that is, without the effort and sacrifice which the white person had to expend.

The facts, of course, are a little different. A high school diploma has been eliminated only for entry to some civil service jobs and promotion, even from these, requires educational preparation; the educational credits demanded of a teacher are still the same but he has somewhat more time to acquire them; the para-professional moves from teacher-aide to teacher assistant to teacher associate and finally to the role of teacher only upon completion of related education, receipt of a degree, and the passing of an examination for a license.

Some concessions, it is true, have been made: the latest civil service ruling grants—with specially ear-marked Federal funds for the salaries involved—to candidates who pass an examination an additional five per cent if they fall within the poverty guidelines for 1968 established by the Office of Economic Opportunity and/or an additional five per cent if they reside in poverty areas (as well as an additional five per cent if they are 55 to 63 years of age); and there is no doubt that colleges are welcoming black students whose high school grades would normally make them ineligible for admission. The argument by the colleges at this point is that they have nowhere near the proportionate number—eleven per cent of the population—of black students in their classrooms, a number hardly to be expected when ghetto schools provided education which, more often than not, had the effect of keeping students from achieving up to their potential. The counter-argument by horrified whites, particularly if they are the liberal whites who manned the political and social barricades of the 1930's, is that they battled once to abolish the evils of a college—or any other—quota system and they will fight again to prevent its reinstitution.

The whites who think this way do not buy the philosophy of preferential treatment at all and refuse to accept any guilt for the past of the American Negro. They may sometimes feel ashamed for not having empathized more with the neglect and struggle of the black man. But that is not quite the same. And perhaps it is better so. Shame is easier to live with than guilt and less likely to end up as the kind of defensive rage which motivates so many of the counter-black revolutionary movements today.

These include the arming by white citizens and police troops for tough law enforcement—which may grow out of fear as well as rage—, the hardening of positions when a white community feels that it is being forced to capitulate (how can one to a Negro?), and the hatred that suddenly fills the white heart when confronting the "arrogant" Negro who does not "know his place," which usually means that the Negro is trying to get ahead, the same as the white person, only a person is more often called dynamic, ambitious, or up-and-coming when he is white. And there is, too, the polarization of attitudes in a black-white confrontation, as in the September, 1968 New York City education crisis. Here, blacks ignored union interests in their concentration on community control over the Ocean Hill-Brownsville schools and whites had no hesitation about forcing into these schools teachers who were considered undesirable by the community governing board and presumably by the community. White reaction to the black parents who tried to block the entrance of the unwanted teachers into the schools was largely, "Who do they think they are?"

Some whites who ask this question and questions like it are spoiling for an out–and–out fight; others withdraw from the confrontation, physically and emotionally, as far as they possibly can. The trek to the suburbs is not only a move to avoid desegregated schools and housing; it is also, and possibly much more so, an escape into a world that is relatively free of black-white issues and challenges and involvements, on one side or another. Happy suburbanites try to forget the black man and his problems, much as many of them did before the black revolution when he was, as far as the general white American consciousness, truly "the invisible man."

A number of these suburbanites are whites who in the old days contributed heavily to Negro charities, led civil rights movements where the black man was supposed to be the prime beneficiary, and invested their money in businesses which serviced, if not entirely to the black man's satisfaction, the ghetto community. But the do-gooders, their intentions, and their check books have been spurned by insolent revolutionaries and the doors of white ghetto businesses are now bolted, either for the duration of the violence or forever. Former feelings of empathy have been shut off, too, as white employers retaliate by demanding that black workers toe the mark and as white parents talk about black propaganda—and black extremist power—taking the place of education.

For the most part, whites—certainly white liberals —react more negatively to some of the tactics of the black revolution than to its cause. And when both sides get irrational, they begin to resemble the patriots of a Fascist state. Blacks impose mob rule, become a law unto themselves, claim moral exemption for violent acts which the white conscience will not tolerate. Whites, putting conscience aside, meet minority demands with tear gas, bullets, and repression. When confrontation reaches this stage, the seeking out of alternatives for deadlocked issues seems pointless.

It appears that few even remember what the original issues were and that only hatred persists.

Actions such as the harassment of white teachers by black parents, the barricading of a city welfare commissioner in his office, the trampling on car tops as part of a demonstration for summer jobs—all of these may offend the white man and stiffen his resistance. But they do not alter the conditions that these actions, no matter how unacceptable, are intended to dramatize: the New York City school system needs to be decentralized and responsible black parents given their opportunity for community control, welfare policies have for years required overhauling, and a massive effort has to be made to provide jobs in ghetto areas where the unemployment rate among the young is as high as forty per cent. These are important social and economic problems. A society that considers itself a democracy has the special obligation of active concern in regard to the problems of its poor—even when some of them are black and their behavior or that of a few of their leaders is not guaranteed to win friends and influence people, particularly white people.

The President's "Riot Commission" made a point of establishing the fact—for blacks it needed no documentation—that virtually every major episode of ghetto unrest in 1967 was foreshadowed by an accumulation of unresolved ghetto grievances against local authorities and that confidence in the willingness and ability of local government to respond to black grievances was low. Blacks usually amend this statement by saying that the confidence is practically nonexistent and further add that local authorities either disregard black grievances or, by ignoring blacks altogether, never even learn what the grievances are. That there is a communications gap between local government and ghetto residents, with resultant feelings of ghetto isolation, alienation, and bitterness which can easily erupt into violence seems, by now, fairly obvious. The means for bridging this separation are not quite so self-evident.

Blacks feel that it is up to the whites to take the next step. They are the haves and the haves are expected to possess a more practical know–how about issues which involve the future of the community. Some unsolicited white condescension may creep into such a relationship but the blacks are probably right. They have both pleaded and demanded. They have made their moves. It is the white man's turn now.

It is furthermore the white man's responsibility—for it is he who is still in charge of the establishment—to initiate the action intended to right the wrongs of ghetto hardship and despair. The gains that have been won as a result of black bludgeoning of the system are sour victories for the black man. They give him no assurance of concern. They leave him with no alternative but to continue his violence in order to achieve the next revolutionary goal and the next and the next. Black headliners may revel in such prospects for orgiastic hatred. Most black leaders believe it is more constructive to avoid the destruction and to work toward including the Negro community as a pluralistic entity in the structure and process of democracy.

The grass roots dialogue can be a start in this direction. It will not be easy. Whites have to face up to the fact that black mistrust has led to almost total rejection not only of white intentions but of the very institutions through which local government functions. Blacks criticize the depersonalization of local services, the inadequacy of existing agencies to cope with black problems, the obliviousness of government function- aries to ghetto sensitivities and to the limitations of ghetto resources for self–help, and perhaps most of all, the practice of excluding blacks from a participating and decision–making role in the planning of ghetto services and development. The chances are that services worked out in cooperation with the intended beneficiaries might be better geared to ghetto needs; if progress turned out to be less than perfect, ghetto leaders could at least dissipate some of the community tensions with explanations which would undoubtedly be more acceptable because they come from ghetto representatives. Something of this sort has been tried in the community action programs of the Economic Opportunity Act. These do not seem to be in current government favor, however.

But dialogue must be initiated if the channels of communication between the black ghetto and the white establishment are ever to be opened. And if some mutual understanding and benefit are to come out of the dialogue, it must be on-going and con- ducted simultaneously with the development—or replanning or refocusing—of the services which have led to the dissatisfactions and the explosions in the first place. The President's "Riot Commission" has recommended neighborhood task forces for this pur- pose and has described in detail both their composi- tion and their operation. Neighborhood leaders, in- cluding representatives of community organizations of all orientations and neighborhood youth leaders, as well as key officials from a mayor's office, ranking city officials from agencies serving a ghetto community, representatives of local business, labor, professional, and church communities, and elected government officers are suggested for membership on a neighborhood task force. The intent is clear: to make possible direct communication between the ghetto and the system. It is further recommended that neighborhood action task forces should meet on a regular basis at a location accessible to ghetto residents, that the chairman of each task force should be the representative from the mayor's office to make absolutely certain of communication with municipal administration, and that in large cities, every chairman of the neighborhood task force should serve on a city-wide task force organized for effective urban action.

In cities where the task force concept has been implemented, considerable dialogue has taken place. All kinds of community groups have come to air their grievances and to externalize their internal frustrations which often have little direct relationship to the problem under discussion. Their vehemence usually subsides when they realize that their gripes are listened to, given thoughtful consideration, and, where possible, acted on immediately. Instructions by the mayor's representative, who sits as chairman of the central task force, to the Commissioner of Police, Sanitation, Buildings, or their representatives, for example, all sitting on the task force, means that parks will be patrolled, abandoned cars picked up, and housing violations inspected. These are functions of the departments involved and no complicated legal action is required to start things moving. When more pressing problems arise, such as community feeling after Dr. King's assassination, an immediate assessment of the tension can be made available by calling together all local task force chairmen for their recommendations about suitable action to the mayor. Or during a hot spell, when hydrants are excessively used by ghetto children to beat the heat, the fire commissioner may use the central task force to alert community task force chairmen about the dangers of a lack of water pressure.

Employment, probably the thorniest grievance of all, is usually on the task force agenda, as are also the many problems of ghetto youth. The resources of the private sector may be involved through the business, labor, professional, and church representation and through the local Urban Coalitions. Needed recreational youth programs can be started or projects worked out for employment or for employment training. During the last year, such programs as play streets, jazzmobiles; trips to the country, to theaters, to concerts, and to sports programs have provided both recreation and varied employment.

The dialogue does not always begin or end with the task force, however. It is just as necessary for a responsible city administration to go out into the streets, to meet the grievances head-on in the civic and tenant and neighborhood organizations that, for reasons of fear or apathy or lack of available representation, do not appear at task force meetings, and to establish a pattern for on-going communication there. It is perhaps even more urgent to provide a forum for the black extremists who scorn a task force as another sellout, who doubt that American government on any level can peaceably be made to move closer or to become more accountable to its black citizens, and who use the catharsis of violence as an unhappy substitute for the organized power that is the right of all groups in a democracy. Their jargon of hatred and abuse may be a new experience for establishment officials accustomed to respect, absolute respect where Negroes are involved. But the import of the black extremist message is not new. It was voiced by a peaceful religious scholar, born in 30 B.C. It was Rabbi Hillel who asked, "If I am not for myself, who is for me? If I am for myself, who am I? If not now, when?"

The black man feels that the white establishment is not for him, that it may never be for him for reasons of conscience or compassion or morality. As he sees it, the interest of the white establishment in making a commitment toward an equal distribution of goods and services and the decision–making process becomes apparent only when the establishment is threatened and the imminent loss exceeds the sacrifice involved in the sharing.

The thinly veiled reference to the destruction of American cities has become a national fear. And white liberals keep looking for alternatives. Many admit that blacks must eventually take their rightful place in the pluralism of American democracy. Some have gone further and conceded to blacks their need to free themselves from the help of the white man so that they can find their own identity and develop their own political and economic strengths as an initial step in meaningful integration. A few have even had enough understanding of black pride to remove themselves from the fringes of the black struggle, somewhat deflating their own egos, no doubt, in the gesture. But most white liberals recoil from the release of democratic restraints that extremist blacks are prone to indulge in and from the "conspiracy" theories with which these and occasionally more moderate groups assault them. It may be that the time for confrontations of this kind is over. Negotiations may be in order now. They have the potential of offering much to both black and white. To the black man, they can be the beginning of a new coalition in which the white man sees him as a partner in a common democratic commitment. To the white, they can mean a deepening of perception which will extend his dimensions as a man.

BIBLIOGRAPHY

Arnez, Nancy. *A Study of Attitudes of Negro Pupils Towards Their Schools.* Journal of Negro Education, Summer 1963.

Ashmore, Harry S. *An Epitaph for Dixie.* New York: W. W. Norton & Co., Inc., 1957.

———. *The Negro and the Schools.* Chapel Hill: University of North Carolina Press, 1954.

Banton, Michael. *Race Relations.* New York: Basic Books, 1968.

Baughman, Emmett Earl. *Negro and White Children.* New York: Academic Press, 1968.

Bennett, LeRone, Jr. *Before the Mayflower.* Baltimore: Penguin Books, 1966.

———. *The Negro Mood.* Chicago: Johnson Publications, 1965.

Blaustein & Zangrando, eds. *Civil Rights and the American Negro.* New York: Washington Square Press, 1966.

Bloom, Richard; Whiteman, Martin; & Deutsch, Martin. *Race and Social Class as Separate Factors Related to Social Environment.* Chicago: The American Journal of Sociology, January 1965.

Bontemps & Conroy. *Anyplace but Here*. New York: Hill & Wang, 1966.

Booker, Simeon. *Black Man's America*. Englewood Cliffs: Prentice Hall, 1964.

Bradin, Anne. *The Wall Between*. New York: Monthly Review Press, 1958.

Brink, William & Harris, Louis. *Black and White: A Study of United States Racial Attitudes Today*. New York: Simon & Schuster, 1967.

———. *The Negro Revolution in America*. New York: Simon & Schuster, 1964.

Broderick, Francis L. & A. Maier, eds. *Negro Protest Thought in the Twentieth Century*. Indianapolis: Bobbs Merrill Co., 1965.

Brown, Claude. *Manchild in the Promised Land*. New York: Signet, 1965.

Chambers, Bradford, ed. *Chronicles of Black Protest*. New York: Mentor, 1968.

Chapman, Abraham, ed. *Black Voices*. New York: New American Library, 1968.

Clark, Kenneth B. *Dark Ghetto: Dilemmas of Social Power*. New York: Harper & Row, 1965.

——— & Mamie P. *The Negro Student at Integrated Colleges*. National Scholarship Service & Fund for Negro Students, 1963.

Cleaver, Eldridge. *Soul on Ice*. New York: Delta, 1968.

Cox, David, ed. and others. *How Does a Minority Group Achieve Power: Case Study of Black Americans*. New York: John Wiley and Sons, Inc., 1969.

Dorman, Michael. *We Shall Overcome*. New York: Dell Publishing Co., 1965.

Drimmer, Melvin, ed. *Black History: A Reappraisal*. Garden City: Doubleday, 1968.

Duberman, Martin B. *In White America*. Boston: Houghton Mifflin, 1964.

DuBois, W.E.B. *Black Reconstruction*. New York: Meridian Books, 1965.

Dykeman, Wilma & Stokely, James. *Neither Black Nor White*. New York: Rinehart & Co., Inc., 1957.

Fanon, Frantz. *The Wretched of the Earth.* New York: Grove Press, 1963.

Franklin, John Hope. *From Slavery to Freedom.* New York: Alfred A. Knopf, Inc., 1956; rev., 1967.

Franklin & Stern, eds. *The Negro in 20th Century America.* New York: Vintage, 1967.

Fulks, Bryan. *Black Struggle: A History of the Negro in America.* New York: Dell, 1969.

Gellhorn, Walter. *American Rights: The Constitution in Action.* New York: Macmillan, 1960.

Ginzberg, Eli. *The Negro Potential.* New York: Columbia University Press, 1956.

——— & Eichner, Alfred. *The Troublesome Presence: American Democracy & The Negro.* New York: Macmillan, 1964.

Ginzburg, Ralph. *100 Years of Lynchings.* New York: Lancer, 1963.

Glazer, Nathan & Moynihan, Daniel P. *Beyond the Melting Pot.* Cambridge: Harvard University Press, 1963.

Gottlieb, David. *Teaching and Students: The Views of Negro and White Teachers.* Sociology of Education, Summer 1964.

Grant, Joanne, ed. *Black Protest.* New York: Fawcett, 1968.

Gregory, Dick. *Nigger.* New York: Dutton, 1964.

Greif, Edward. *The Silent Pulpit.* New York: Holt, Rinehart, and Winston, 1964.

Grier, William H. and Cobbs, Price M. *Black Rage.* New York: Basic Books, 1969.

Griffin, J. H. *Black Like Me.* New York: Signet, 1960.

Habe, Hans. *The Wounded Land: Journey Through a Divided America.* New York: Coward-McCann, 1964.

Handlin, Oscar. *The Newcomers: Negroes and Puerto Ricans in a Changing Metropolis.* Washington, D.C.: Howard University Press, 1959.

Hentoff, Nat. *The New Equality.* New York: Viking, 1964.

Herton, Calvin C. *Sex and Racism in America.* New York: Grove Press, Inc., 1965.

Humphrey, Hubert H., ed. *Integration vs. Segregation: The Crisis in Our Schools as Viewed by 17 Outstanding Commentators.* New York: Crowell, 1964.

Jones, LeRoi. *Blues People*. New York: William Morrow and Co., Inc., 1963.

Jordan, Winthrop D. *White Over Black: American Attitudes Toward the Negro, 1550–1812*. Chapel Hill: University of North Carolina Press, 1968.

King, Martin Luther. *Stride Toward Freedom: The Montgomery Story*. New York: Harper & Row, 1958.

———. *Why We Can't Wait*. New York: Harper, 1964.

LaFarge, John. *The Catholic Viewpoint on Race Relations*. Garden City: Doubleday, 1956.

Lester, Julius. *Look Out, Whitey! Black Power's Going Get Your Mama*. New York: Dial Press, Inc., 1968.

Lewis, Anthony & The New York Times. *Portrait of a Decade: The Second American Revolution*. New York: Bantam, 1965.

Lincoln, D. Eric. *The Black Muslims in America*. Boston: Beacon Press, 1961.

Lomax, Louis E. *The Negro Revolt*. New York: Harper & Row, 1962.

Lubell, Samuel. *White and Black : Test of a Nation*. New York: Harper & Row, 1964.

Meier, August. *From Plantation to Ghetto*. New York: Hill and Wang, 1966.

Meltzer, Milton, ed. *In Their Own Words: A History of the American Negro*. New York: Crowell, 1965.

Moody, Anne. *Coming of Age in Mississippi*. New York: Dial, 1968; New York: Dell, 1969.

Muse, Benjamin. *Ten Years of Prelude*. New York: Viking, 1964.

Olsen, Jack. *Black is Best: The Riddle of Cassius Clay*. New York: Dell, 1967.

Osofsky, Gilbert. *Harlem: the Making of a Ghetto*. New York: Harper & Row, 1963.

Peck, James. *Freedom Ride*. New York: Simon & Schuster, 1962.

Perlo, Victor. *Empire of High Finance*. New York: International Publishers, 1965.

Quarles, Benjamin. *The Negro in the Making of America*. New York: Collier, 1964.

Raab, Earl, ed. *American Race Relations Today*. Garden City: Doubleday, 1962.

Randel, William P. *The Ku Klux Klan: A Century of Infamy*. Philadelphia: Chilton, 1965.

Rathbun, Georgiana. *Revolution in Civil Rights*. Congressional Quarterly Service, 1968.

Rowan, Carl Thomas. *Go South to Sorrow*. New York: Random House, 1957.

Savage, Henry. *Seeds of Time: The Background of Southern Thinking*. New York: Holt, 1959.

Silberman, Charles E. *Crisis in Black and White*. New York: Random House, 1964.

Silver, James W. *Mississippi: The Closed Society*. New York: Harcourt, Brace & World, 1964.

Stone, Chuck. *Black Political Power in America*. Indianapolis: Bobbs Merrill, 1968; New York: Delta, 1970.

Stringfellow, William. *My People is the Enemy*. New York: Holt, Rinehart, and Winston, 1964.

Weinstein, Allen & Gatell, Frank Otto, eds. *American Negro Slavery: A Modern Reader*. New York: Oxford University Press, 1968.

Weaver, Robert C. *Negro Labor: A National Problem*. Port Washington: Kennikat Press, Inc., 1946.

Westin, Alan F. *Freedom Now! The Civil Rights Struggle in America*. New York: Basic Books, 1964.

Wills, Garry. *The Second Civil War: Arriving for Armageddon*. New York: The New American Library, 1968.

Index

Community action pro-
grams, 7-8, 160-74, 198
See also Economic Op-
portunity Act
Community control, *see* Decentralization; *specific
schools*
Community Corporations,
128
Community Development
Agency, 164
Confrontation, provocation
for, 136-37, 144
Congress of Racial Equality
(CORE), 99, 102, 119,
182
headquarters of, 9
Jewish support of, 133
as peace makers, 84
philosophy of, 39-40
walk-out of, 46
Consumer education, 126-
27, 163, 165
Conyers, John, 149, 152
Cooperative buying clubs,
127
Council Against Poverty,
162-65
Council of Supervisory Associations, 101
Countee Cullen Library, 93

Daley, Mayor, 142
Davis, Sammy, Jr., 69
Dawson, William, 149, 151-
52
Debray, Regis, 137, 141
Decentralization, 1, 6-7, 40,

42, 95-106, 128, 168, 180,
196
Declaration of Indepen-
dence, guarantees of, 60
Democratic party
conventions of, 156, 158
members of, 149, 152-53
Detroit, 149, 152
riot control in, 137, 141,
142
schools of, 86, 92, 104
Diggs, Charles, 149, 152
Disabled unemployables, 20
Dixiecrat-Republican coalition, 158
Dropouts, school, 23, 38
Drug addiction, 73, 76, 181

Economic boycotts, 41
Economic development, program for, 62, 64, 71-72
Economic Opportunity Act,
6-8, 70-71, 160-74, 191,
196
See also Office of Eco-
nomic Opportunity
Education
by blacks, 29, 58-69
compensatory, 62-64, 69-
71, 80, 94
equal opportunity of, 39,
154
equivalency classes, 62-63
importance of, 52-54, 192
youth in, 77-79
See also Schools
Education and Labor Com-
mittee, 152
Egypt, 27